To Wess —

A very dear frien[d]
who someday will
provide the best chapter
of this Book!

(Best wishes —

with love

[signature]

January 1980

male
model

male model

THE WORLD BEHIND THE CAMERA

charles hix

with michael taylor

DESIGNED BY BRIAN BURDINE

ST. MARTIN'S PRESS
New York

Library of Congress Cataloging in Publication Data

Hix, Charles.
  Male model.

  Includes index.
  1. Models, Fashion—United States.   2. Employment of
men—United States.   I. Taylor, Michael Byron, joint
author.   II. Title.
HD8039.M772U54   659.1'52   79-16546
ISBN 0-312-50938-3

From both of us—
To the models
who said it
and gave us a book
To the photographers
especially Albert, Barry, Bruce, Ken and Les
who recorded the images
To Vicky, Elise, Peggy and Jill
who dug in
To Brian
and his eyes
From Michael—
To Gayle
with love
From Chuck—
To Bob
my friend and back-up
From each other—
To each other
hugs

*Michael Ives
Photo:
Bruce Weber*

CHAPTERS

sizing up

While we barely noticed, male modeling unfolded into a multi-million-dollar business.

As more and more male models stared us squarely in the face from newspapers, magazines and highway billboards, we couldn't evade their presence any longer. Nor could we dismiss the world of male modeling as a frivolous realm. By the end of 1978, several top model agencies reported that their men's divisions were pulling in nearly a third of their total profits, an energetic leap from approximately 10 percent only five years earlier. Although the field was still dominated by females who commanded the top dollars, a dozen or so guys in the uppermost echelon of male modeling were making $100,000 and upward annually. Beginning male models could get $75 an hour selling their faces in the world's major modeling city, New York.

The rise (with no fall in sight) of male modeling is even more remarkable when one considers its questionable reputation. Still, despite the slurs and the sneers, the evidence is clear: our images of maleness are changing, and models are involved in the transformations.

Since print advertising began, male models have been around selling suspenders and hair creams. But only a few—very few—isolated men made their living modeling. Modeling was a sideline, seldom particularly lucrative. Male models were considered akin to sideshow freaks, curiosities drifting far outside the mainstream.

During the thirties and forties, when *Esquire* was its most influential, that magazine presented men's fashions mainly in drawings, infrequently in photographs with professional models. So there was a sprinkling of modeling jobs for men, but the field remained mostly a desert. Meanwhile, female modeling flourished. Even during the fifties and well into the sixties, the male image in fashion advertising was studied and stiff.

Contact sheet & print
Matt Leddick & child
Photo: Palma Kolansky

The typical male model (still a part-timer) worked more often, but in his pictures he was little more than a cardboard mannequin. His rigidity reflected our rigid perception of maleness—Rational Man contrasted with Emotional Woman, Superior Man versus Inferior Woman.

Then, our time-honored images of maleness (and femaleness) encountered some startling reinterpretations. We'd already been rocked by Elvis when the Beatles took us on new trips. Suddenly the man in the gray flannel suit put on Nehru jackets and love beads. The collegiate went hippy and Yippie. The complacency of "We Like Ike" was replaced by slogans of discontent. Watts burned and we went to the moon. We lived through Vietnam and survived Nixon. The feminist and the gay rights movements took to the streets and challenged our views of sexual identity. We didn't know all the answers anymore, but we sure as hell had a lot more questions. We began to question the arbitrary distinctions between maleness and femaleness. Was wearing cologne really womanly? Was long hair really feminine? Designers of women's clothing began designing for men. Both fashion and Madison Avenue rediscovered the male market. And the man in the street got confused.

As our vision of the world and where we fit into it became less secure, we turned increasingly inward. We turned to *us*, to *our* feelings, looking for *our* answers, not hand-me-down truths. One of the manifestations of this introspection was a greater concern with how we looked. Looking into ourselves, we also looked more clearly at ourselves.

It is not a coincidence that male models stepped out of the shadows while we were preoccupied with what seemed weightier matters. We weren't aware that we were calling upon models to sell us alternative self-views. When we bought the shirts and liquor and blue jeans and cigarettes that the models were advertising, we told ourselves that we were only buying the products. But we were also buying something else —an image of what the American male should look like. Which is ironic, because now we claim that male models don't properly represent *us*. Of course they do. If we didn't buy their goods and their looks, male models would simply disappear. Hard-nosed businessmen do not hire models out of charitable sentiments. They hire models because models deliver the goods—substantial profits. We buy, literally and figuratively, what the models are selling.

No wonder the world of male modeling is contradictory to its core. It is founded on our own contradictions. Analogies can be made to other worlds—the flesh-and-fantasy world of movies or the trick-us-if-you-can world of the magician—but the comparisons only go so far.

Like both the actor and the magician, the model deals in illusion. When Christopher Reeve soars through the air as Superman or when another caped man performs sleight of hand, we know we're being hoodwinked. Just as we know that the man in the magazine strolling through an emerald field in a Harris tweed suit isn't taking his daily constitutional. These are all staged events.

Michael Edwards
Photo: Albert Watson

Jeff Aquilon
Photo: Bruce Weber

As a society, we have developed no extended mythology surrounding the magician as magician. We are perfectly content to forget about him once he leaves the stage. The model's illusion represents something more mysterious. His magic is beyond our grasp. We create visions not only of his professional life but of his off-camera existence as well. We fabricate fictions for the male model to live out, publicly and privately, in our imaginings. For our own purposes.

In this way, the model's world is closer to the actor's. In America, our self-images have always been strongly influenced by movie heroes so secure in our collective consciousness that many of them don't even require first names. When Gable took off his shirt in *It Happened One Night* and revealed his bare chest, the sale of men's undershirts dropped with a thud. Brando did great things for black leather jackets in *The Wild One*. Redford wore a pink suit in *The Great Gatsby* and brought back thirties men's fashions in the seventies. Travolta took white vested suits to every disco in the country following *Saturday Night Fever*.

The model's effect is less immediately dramatic. He works more slowly, more cumulatively, but the results are generally longer lasting. The *Gatsby* and the *Saturday Night Fever* clothing crazes died quickly. But the European-shaped suit—considered radical when first introduced —set a men's fashion style for a decade. The more we see models wearing new clothing styles, the more our eyes become accustomed to changing styles and to changes in the male image.

In the long run, models may have a more profound impact on the way American men look than our heroes of the cinema. Although we use movie stars and models in much the same way—we compare ourselves to them—there is a critical difference in our responses to actors and models.

Actors are people we know. Their names are on marquees, we talk and gossip about them as individuals. We have a more accessible relationship with actors than with models. Models are anonymous celebrities. We may recognize their faces, but we seldom know their names. We see them on the printed page, voiceless and immobile. Whatever personality a model has is one we give him. Usually we take the lazy route and endow all male models with the same traits.

We stereotype models and we glorify actors because we want something from both. From the actor, we want all he has to offer—his fame, his glamor, his salary, his lifestyle, his everything. From the model, we want only his looks. The fantasies we extract from the model's flesh are deeper, more illusive, because the process of assimilating the model into our lives is quirky and far more vague than emulating an actor.

Male models do their jobs well. They sell the aftershave lotion and they sell us on the complex notion that if we douse ourselves with the fragrance, we too will be chased by a bevy of sex-starved sex objects. The model is a stand-in for a fantasized version of ourselves.

We make actors and models bigger than life to make ourselves larger. We're momentarily happiest when we have a whole galaxy of stars—folk and pop heroes, jock heroes, cult personalities, this-and-that figures—to empathize with. They don't manipulate us. We manipulate them. We infuse them with mythic power and elevate them out of our reach.

But we're not total fools. We have some objectivity. The worlds shown in the movies, the worlds depicted in the magazines—we know those worlds are not real. We just wish they were. And that we were the main characters living smack dab in the middle of them. But we're not. And plainly, we're not living the lives our heroes lead. Despite all the fantasies, we haven't become them, so they have failed us. Secretly, we wish them a fall from grace. To get the dirt on actors, we turn to sensational tabloids. With no access to the inside scoop on nameless models, we rely on our stereotypes to discount them: male models are all stupid, superficial and gay.

But they are not that easily dismissed. Let's face facts. Beauty may be only skin deep, but has anyone not wished to be more attractive? Sure, we'd also like brilliant minds and lots of charm. However, if push could ever come to shove, *inside*, armies of us would opt for the surface trapping first. It's only recently that we've gotten the nerve to admit that men do care—a lot—about how they look. Many decry what they call the new narcissism of today's male. Vanity, they say, is a female trait, and they foresee the downfall of Western Civilization in the avowal that men, too, want to look good. These doomsters are wrong. Men are only becoming more honest.

In the mid-sixties, the standard for the male model was a conservatively mid-American appearance. That image reinforced the established view of the male as Breadwinner and Family Man. A little stolid but very solid.

By and large, the current crop of male models is characterized by a sporty, energetic, healthy appearance. That reflects the high priority currently given to youthful vigor, to working out and staying fit. But while the athletic look is predominant, it is by no means unrivaled. Offering competition is the suave look, the sensual look, the mean and the macho look. The male image is more diverse than it once was, possibly because we're beginning to realize that maleness is more diversified than we once thought.

But many people have difficulty perceiving how male modeling relates to a *real* man. In our society, we have always associated modeling with women. And because our society was founded on male-is-supreme sexism, anything associated with the female sex is *prima facie* inferior. Male models have therefore been assigned inferior social and professional status.

It is characteristic of attitudes about male modeling that the gender qualifier is constantly used. In an article entitled "The Second Sex"

Craig Vandenburgh
Photo: Ken Haak

(April 10, 1978), *Newsweek* noted the inroads made by prominent male models in recent years, but concluded, "Even with their new equality, there's still a long way to go before the male model becomes a male role model," ignoring the fact that female models have never served as female role models, nor have they been expected to.

But male models, like female models, do more. They offer us a repertoire of images to try out mentally and emotionally. Every image of maleness is valid, just as every image of femaleness is valid. We are all potentially all other people.

Male models are human beings too. Muddling through is what consumes most of our energy. Like everybody else, male models have a lot of muddle to get through, because they *are* "everybody else." Like all of us, they resent being pigeonholed. None of us wants to be written off before we have a chance to prove our worth, and models are not exceptions. In terms of Ultimate Significance, modeling doesn't score high. Few things do. If we asked the same sort of question—how do models contribute to the greater good?—of our own jobs, most of us would flunk. The criterion is utopian. Like us, models are earthbound. Like us, they want to be loved. They prefer not to look full-face at society's ambivalence toward them and their work. Most male models take heart in the fact that they have become visible and vocal on television programs and in newspaper and magazine articles, where they've talked about their career as a profession, not as an embarrassment. Many want to believe that their battle for respectability has been won. In fact, they are not clear-cut victors. Their tarnished image still persists and their coverage has usually been patronizing.

In researching this book, I found that most of the male models interviewed were willing to tell the whole and nothing but the truth. But it was the truth as they saw it. Or wanted to see it. Nearly without exception, the models interviewed wanted to vindicate themselves and their profession.

It is human nature to pretend, and maybe to be convinced, that small gains, or even large ones, have been vaster than the territory truly annexed. There is little jubilation over a truce when part of the newly-won ground remains pocked with landmines or other explosive material.

To some, the foregoing analogy must seem melodramatic. But when I began this book, I found myself in the midst (to my eyes) of a fray between models (whether or not they were militant) and a too-often derisive public. Sometimes I felt cornered. Should I write *my* version? Or should I write the models'? I understood their desire to appear decisively triumphant, and I didn't want to be deemed a traitor. As one of the characters in this story says, "Rejection is nowhere for anybody."

Ultimately, I made my separate peace. I would present a verbal portrait of the industry and of the people in it, as often as possible in their own words. But when my writer's instincts informed me that those

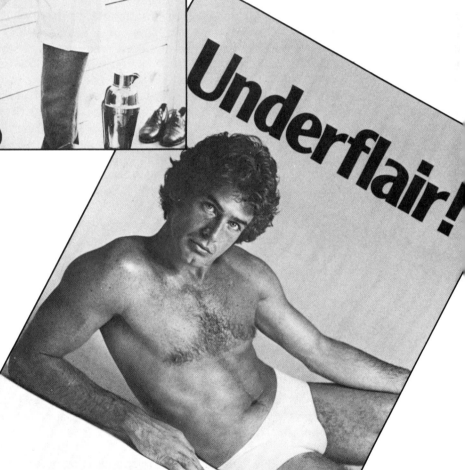

Tony Sanchez (top), Photo: Barry Kaufman. Jack Scalia in a breakthrough ad for men's underwear. Photo: Francesco Scavullo. Courtesy of Eminence International.

Underflair!

words were self-serving and presented a rosier picture than the facts warranted, I'd intercede with my own gray vision of reality.

In maintaining my perspective, I had a great boost from my collaborator, Michael Taylor, a successful model working both coasts for over a decade. He conducted nearly as many interviews as I, in addition to bringing with him experiences that I could never have lived or uncovered. Together, we amassed thousands of pages of transcripts. But Michael's assistance was even more significant on another plane. He never shied away from tapping his own feelings, and his introspection was invaluable. His remarks communicate his experiences—and very rich ones—though they are not meant to be taken as representative of all models. We decided his personal observations should precede several of the chapters, so Michael could comment in his own voice on the subjects up for discussion.

While I was writing this book, I would have preferred to ignore, or at least sweep tidily aside, the subject of homosexuality. At the outset, I felt little was to be gained from thrashing a dead horse. Even though rumor has it that every male model is either a homosexual or a closet case, statement after statement has been made to refute the assertion. An article in the New York *Daily News* once listed the guesses of people who *might* know the percentages of gays versus straights in the business (although how they would know I can't imagine). Ludicrously, the estimates ranged from 10 to 90 percent gay. I wanted to discount the question because it is not legitimate, and it's a loaded one to boot. Like an actor, a model must convey a persona in his work. Unlike an actor, he usually has only his physical being to work with, since he deals with the printed image and seldom the spoken word. What the model projects is what counts. How the projection is interpreted depends a great deal on the onlooker's preconceptions. On many occasions I have heard particular viewers state that a model looks gay when I know the model is straight, and vice versa.

Like it or not, fair or not, homosexuality is a recurring theme in any view of male modeling. It colors how society looks upon the profession and how models' psyches are affected by becoming models. During every interview it kept asserting itself, usually against the wishes of all parties concerned. Only when homosexuality is no longer seen as reprehensible will male models be seen as totally respectable. *Not* because all or even a sizable majority of male models are gay. And *not* because gayness or straightness is a valid criterion when evaluating job performance: as the line goes in the ranks, "You're only as good as your last picture." The reason lays bare a worrisome truth—our society assumes any extraordinarily good-looking man is gay and has associated male modeling with homosexuality for so long that the two subjects are forced bedfellows.

Still, a mystique surrounds the anonymous celebrities whose faces are familiar but whose names and lives are seldom known. They are glamorous. Or so their ambivalent public believes. Anticipating the assault that's become historic—glamor, like money, corrupts—most models take cover by proclaiming, "I am a businessman, a salesman. That's all modeling is about, selling products. I just happen to be my own product." Stepping lively to duck the allegation that they lead undeservedly glamorous lives, they try to make themselves invincible to such criticism by deglamorizing themselves. Guess what. Society won't let them.

Modeling *is* glamorous. *And* it is mundane. It's fraught with paradox. Some models are brilliant. Some are fools. Some are warm and humane. Others are creeps. I've tried to present their world, not as it's commonly supposed to be, but as I see it. With warts. Also with a face that is sometimes radiant.

The fellows who decide to take a fling at modeling expect to bask only in the radiance. They haven't yet been introduced to the world behind the camera.

Journalist Kazuko Aso styles shoeless model Tony Lago's trousers during photography session. Photo: Peter Sakas

breaking in

The first thing I ever remember wanting to be was an actor. My brother and I were living with a Seventh-Day Adventist family. My parents had separated, so this family took care of us on their farm in Ohio. We lived there for four years. I was ten or so when I saw my first movie. We drove into the city—Marietta, Ohio—about fifty miles away, and it was a big occasion. After I saw the movie—*The Mighty Joe Young* with Terry Moore and a big gorilla, and the hero, I think, was Ben Johnson—well, that cinched it. That's when I decided that what I needed to do in the world was act.

I didn't tell a soul. But I did go around re-creating the whole movie on the farm. For months and months. I acted every role. The gorilla. Terry Moore. The hero. I did them all.

I never wanted to be anything other than an actor. But when I was still living on the farm, we used to get the Sears Roebuck catalogs. I would go through them, page by page, on winter evenings sitting in front of the big potbellied stove, and I would look at the pictures. I thought they were really beautiful people, not really *real* people, but whoever they were, they were very beautiful.

In high school, I took an acting class, but I treated it as a joke. I told my counselors and teachers that I wanted to be a psychologist. That sounded pretty good. In college (California State University at Northridge), for the first time I really committed myself to wanting to be an actor. I studied drama intensively and other subjects not at all. I would get A's in drama and D's in anthropology and psychology, so it would average out and I could stay in school.

Michael Taylor, 1979
Photo: Les Goldberg

While I was doing a play in college—it was 1962—the director (also a student) mentioned that he modeled some to help finance his going to college. He suggested that I try it. Which came as a surprise. I didn't think people who modeled had anything to do with the real people I knew in the world. I'd look at their pictures but I didn't know their names. They had no personality, no *life*, attached to them. I asked the guy what someone did to model. He gave me the name of a photographer, whom I went to, thinking, What a great idea!

The photographer told me to bring several different outfits—a tennis outfit, a collegiate-type outfit, a suit, and a sweater and slacks. We shot on a tennis court. We shot on horseback. We did head shots. I felt wonderful. I had no idea what I was doing but I wasn't at all concerned. I just thought, My, this is great fun. I overdid everything. It was a very expressive shooting, shall we say. The photographer couldn't believe a person could move so much, and so fast. He was very encouraging and I thought I had the secret. I didn't.

The photographer called the Flaire Agency in Los Angeles, so did my friend, and they set up an appointment for me. I had to borrow money from my folks to pay for the photographs. Sixty dollars. My folks thought it was just about the silliest thing they'd ever heard of. They were all confused, because they did think something was in the air: supposedly I was going to be a psychologist, and here I was doing all these plays in school and not going to my psychology classes. But they lent me the money anyway.

The appointment was at the agency in Beverly Hills. I borrowed my mom's car. Mine wasn't working. I was very nervous.

I took two sport jackets that I'd had forever. But I thought they were quite stylish. I shaved and covered up the nicks. I greased back my hair with Brilliantine. I thought I looked very, very dashing, exactly like a model should look. The jacket was ill-fitting. The pants were too short. I looked like a gawky kid. Ignorance is bliss.

I drove to the agency. It was a little house, a very well done little house, sitting on Sunset Boulevard in Beverly Hills. It had very plush carpeting. There was a receptionist. I spoke in whispered tones, asking, "Is Mr. Chan here?" His name, in fact, was Chan something-or-other. She said, "Please have a seat." I felt like I was in a doctor's office.

He came out and said, "Michael?" I said, "Yes," still barely audible. He said, "Come in, please." He was very elegant, soft-spoken, quite charming, and I got even more nervous because I was not any of those things. I think I rather amused him. He said he'd heard good reports about me from the photographer and that he'd like to see the pictures. I'd brought along the contact sheet. He said, "Well, you

Three-year-old Michael (upper left); after seeing Mighty Joe Young, *young Taylor decided to become an actor (upper right); at the high school junior prom (far left);* High *school graduation portrait, 1961 (lower right).*

know, you have a good look, but you're young." But he thought
that I could work and decided to take me with the agency.

He gave me his phone number and said to check in. He didn't
talk about anything. He told me to get some of the pictures blown up
and that we'd go from there. And from there we went nowhere.

Six weeks later, I called him, very irate, asking, "What is going on?"
He said, "Nothing." I remember saying, "Do you really, in fact,
want me with your agency?" He said, "Yes, I do." I said, "Oh, fine,
okay. Good-bye." And then I would call him regularly every six
weeks and I would be irate and he would say, "Yes, I want you with
the agency," and I'd say, "Great, good-bye." I just assumed that's the
way the modeling business went.

After my second year at college, I joined the navy. During that
time, I never had a modeling assignment.

—*M.T.*

A photo from Taylor's first professional shooting.
As a result, he joined the Flaire agency in L.A.

While male models are often envied but seldom respected, more American men than ever before ache to see their picture in the papers and are heading toward agency doors. Joey Hunter, an executive with Ford Men in New York City, conservatively estimates that about five men without a hint of modeling experience contact that agency daily. Zoli—his last name is never used in business—heads another major New York agency, Zoli Men, and every week is contacted by thirty-five to fifty men intent on breaking into the field. Nina Blanchard, who directs the agency bearing her name in Los Angeles, notes that she hears from eight or ten new aspirants every working day. In San Francisco at the Grimmé Agency, owner Jimmy Grimmé receives nearly a dozen pictures each day from male hopefuls.

Statistically, chances for success are abysmal.

Hunter: "I would say of brand-new men in any four-month period I would take on two or three. I do take maybe four or five over that four-month period who either come from another agency or from Europe, men I find in Europe or California. I go to Europe once a year, to California two or three times a year. I go down to Texas, to Denver, and I look for models. But as far as brand-new people, guys who don't have one professional picture, I would say two every four months."

Zoli: "I have about sixty male models now, a collection gathered over the years. I might take on ten or twelve new men in the course of a year. Not more than half will have the stamina to see the whole thing through until it becomes financially rewarding. A rough guess for the median income of working male models would be between thirty and forty thousand a year. Of course, a lot never make that and only about a dozen guys in this business earn anything near the hundred-thousand-dollar mark from print."

Blanchard: "Once, only once in the last year have I seen or interviewed anybody who sent his picture in. Usually the good ones come recommended by photographers, or maybe an agent has said something to them. We don't take on that many new ones. California doesn't have that much editorial or that much fashion work. So the new guys we take on have to have some potential as actors and be able to work in commercials. Say we try out maybe twenty or so new guys a year. Maybe two will work out."

Grimmé: "It's eleven o'clock. Since nine-thirty, I've already personally interviewed about ten people this morning. I have not taken any. None. A young kid walked in the other day, a friend of a model, which cuts no ice with me whatsoever. If I can't make money off someone, he can't make money off me, and then there's no sense in building up false hopes just to have a picture on the wall. But another young boy walked in the other day with no pictures. I very seldom do this, but I took him without even seeing a snapshot. Rare. Very, very rare."

The market is always glutted by the number of would-be male models. Although there is much more work than a decade or even five years ago, there's not enough for all the men hungry for a piece of the pie.

The prodding of others—lovers, strangers, occasionally someone in the business—generally triggers modeling ambitions. Or allows the ambition to be voiced and acted upon.

Ted Dawson, considered by most insiders to be the premier model of the last two decades, offers a somewhat typical story, but one with an unusual backdrop. "I started in Australia. I knew a girl there who went on to be a very famous model in Europe and New York in the sixties. We were kids together, friends, and I had just bought a car and didn't have enough money to pay for it. I was working for a shipping company, a very straitlaced English shipping company. She said, 'Model on your lunch hour,' and I started doing it. I was making more between one and two than I was from nine to five for a five-day week. Another girl I knew, another great beauty, went to London and became a big model on the Continent." Having decided to follow their examples and to try modeling full time, "I fought with my family and left them feeling very despondent. I left for Europe. My first job, I got the equivalent of eight or nine dollars an hour. I had been in London a week, three days working with a magazine, and I thought I was the richest person in the world."

Bill Loock, affectionately called the granddaddy of the business, was introduced to modeling by a fluke. After his discharge from the air corps early in 1945, he joined his father's insurance business. "Modeling was not the most respectable way to make a buck in those days," he recalls. He was lunching with a client who had to drop off a package at a photographer's studio. In the tradition of the silver screen, the photographer asked Loock if he'd ever modeled. Loock said no but posed for a couple of quick shots, which the photographer sent to an agent.. "I was the first model to have an Ivy League identification, and it worked. But I never left the insurance business. I knew modeling was a precarious field, and I needed the self-discipline of something to do when not modeling. Besides, I was married and had four kids right away."

Matt Collins, the cover model for *Looking Good* who has been called the first superstar male model, was discovered at Madison Square Garden while he was showing horses. (Collins was enjoying a lucrative career as a trainer and had been described as Olympic material for the equestrian events.) His mentor was New York agent Wilhelmina, herself a former model and head of the successful Wilhelmina agency. When she remarked that he—and she—could make millions off his cheekbones, "I thought she was a groupie," Collins is fond of recalling. But he quickly went to her office.

Joe MacDonald's first national ad, shot by the famous photographer Victor Skrebneski, turned out to be the back of his head. "After college,

Ted Dawson (left) first modeled in Australia during his lunch hours. Photo: Les Goldberg. From this shooting, the picture of Matt Collins (right) was selected for the cover of Looking Good. *Photo: Bruce Weber*

I sold my car and stereo and took one of those Icelandic Airways trips to Europe," he relates. "I'd spent three months in Europe and ended up in Paris with almost no money. I was planning to go to Paris Planning [a modeling agency there], and that same day I was out walking and I saw these two guys across the street looking at me. Then they crossed the street, and I thought, Oh-oh. They said they'd like to do a picture of me the next day, could they see my teeth? I thought, my *teeth*? So I smiled, thinking it was going to be pornography for sure. They were going to pay me $200 to show my teeth? Come on. So I went to the studio. In fact, the photographer was very good. The funniest part about getting the job was that they actually did want unknown people. But the campaign didn't come out for two years. By then, I was like a star in Paris. I had billboards for Eminence underwear. I was on the cover of *Marie Claire*. I did all the men's *Vogue* stuff. Then the toothpaste poster came out. It was so stupid. I had a rose coming out of my mouth

because Close-Up Toothpaste made my breath so sweet. Something ridiculous. So it was really funny."

Jack Mayhall, one of Dallas's more successful models with the Kim Dawson Agency, first heard the suggestion that he should model while he was standing at a urinal.

"I was at an alumni party, and a lady who works at Kim's was there too," recalls Mayhall. "I didn't know her at the time. Well, she was at the party and she saw me and she got a friend of hers to meet me in the men's room. He waited till I went to the bathroom. There I was at the urinal. And somebody says, 'Would you like to be a model?' Yeah, sure. And he said, 'No, seriously,' and he went into this big thing saying how he had been coerced into going in there and talking to me. And he had her name and number and all that sort of thing, and he said that I should give her a call. Well, I thought it would be kind of interesting and fun to do. I went into it as kind of a whim, a part-time job to do something fun and make some spending money. So I called her one day and saw her and that is how I got started. In the bathroom. While I was going to the bathroom."

If one believes models' professed stories, only a soul or two ever felt a burning desire from childhood, or even puberty, to be photographed with an eye patch in a Hathaway shirt. Many models *say* that they first checked out the scene as kind of a goof. Few claim they ever saw modeling as a calling. A sizable number of guys gravitated toward a modeling career because they had no clear conception of what else they wanted to do or because it seemed more attractive than a humdrum or other-

(Left) Joe MacDonald's first ad pictured the back of his head. Photo: Loíc Raout. Jack Mayhall (right) was approached about modeling in a rest room. Photo: Thomas Sofield

wise objectionable job. The profession is dotted with ex-teachers, ex-salesmen, ex-dropouts. And at least one ex-Illinois state trooper. Chicago-based Don Guide describes the circumstances that led him to modeling:

"In early 1974—around January, February—I was working on an expressway in the early morning hours. I saw this car parked in the middle of the expressway, in the right lane. I pulled up, stopped and got out. The driver was, naturally, intoxicated. In the meantime, somebody was approaching from the rear, which I didn't know, somebody who never saw me. The driver was on bennies and was cruising sixty-five right toward my car and the other guy's car. I happened to look up when he was about a car length away from my car. I made a break for the side of the road. I made it; I'm here. But after that accident, I figured my time was running low and that I had to find other work. So I figured I'd stop downtown. My mother was trying to get me off the job, she thought it was too dangerous. She suggested I see an agent my sister had been registered with once. I did go see him, asked him if I could make some money in the business and he said I could. So I quit my job. In the meantime, his agency folded. So I walked into A Plus [one of Chicago's top agencies, especially for men] and got signed up and I've been with them ever since. My first year I was starving."

Modeling's ranks also include an ex-amateur boxer whose friendliness with a police photographer got him started. "I boxed for about five or six years, I guess," tells Jerry Gustin. "In the summer, they have leagues set up. Friday nights, you go down and they throw you in the ring. You aren't considered a pro or nothing, but they give you something. I used to fight a lot when I was growing up in Camden, New Jersey. A tough area. A lot of race riots. Boxing was safer. You were not on the streets. I went to California and did some construction work. Saved some money and enrolled in college. A girl I met in college got me involved in modeling. She worked at a police station taking mug shots. That was her job and that was her hobby, photography. We started doing some stuff and she got me in a contest for *Playgirl* "Discovery of the Month" or something like that. She sent some nude pictures in. I didn't even know what she was doing with them. So *Playgirl* wanted their photographer to do some nude stuff of me. The shots really came out nice and were going to go into the magazine and everything. I took the pictures and the photographer told me I should go see Tom Hahn at Mary Webb Davis. When I got to the agency, I was told it would be better if I didn't pose nude if I wanted to be a real model. So *Playgirl* didn't publish the pictures. I never got the money or anything. Just had nice pictures sitting on the shelf, you know."

Most aspirants are totally ignorant of what the career encompasses. They vaguely consider modeling a glamorous, make-it-rich-quick business awaiting them with open arms and open pockets. They believe the

only requisite is a handsome face. The more sophisticated contact modeling agencies directly. The more naïve hie themselves to the nearest modeling school they have seen advertised in their local newspapers.

Asked her opinion of modeling schools for men, Nina Blanchard raises her eyes and her voice. "Modeling schools for women are bad enough. Modeling schools for men are worse," the agent insists, striking her desk top with scarlet fingernails. Of males who've finished the curriculum, Blanchard says, "First of all, they're very mannered. The people who teach in those schools, I've never known one who has been a knowledgeable male model, who was successful. Many of the guys teaching in the schools I'm familiar with are, well, just tired old acting queens. They end up teaching the guys all wrong, how to do turns on the runway and stuff like that. And the guys that go to them, they're the guys that most agencies wouldn't touch with a ten-foot pole anyway. And I'm talking about even the small towns. I think that a good grooming course on how to clear the pimples on your face, cut your hair and stay out of polyester pant suits is far better than any modeling course a guy could have. They're not going to make a model out of you. If you don't have it, no school can help you. If you have it, you don't need a school. It's that simple. Schools are just anathema, they're just really terrible."

Although Blanchard is more vehement than most, her sentiments about schools, particularly franchised operations, are shared by many professionals in the business. And a school that comes under much criticism is Barbizon modeling school for men. It has also been sharply called to task by a former employee with many years in the modeling school business. While employed at Barbizon in New York City, she was forbidden to discuss any company policies with the press. Mary, as we'll call her, claims that she could no longer put up with the blatant hype spewed by a school where, in her words, "Anybody who has the money is accepted. That's the only criterion—money." Although she occasionally exhibits moral outrage, most often she speaks slowly and sadly in a monotone.

"Barbizon wanted to cash in on the growing market for male models, so they started the school for men a couple years ago, doing it very, very quickly. They took from the female course those things that they thought they could incorporate into a male program. They deleted fancy names, like the Dior Spin or the Dior Crossover, and they just called them, like, the quarter-turn or the half-turn, things like that. (Well, you can't really teach a man how to walk, because as soon as you do, he loses his masculinity.) Frankly, I don't think that you can *teach* a man to be a male model. Someone either has it or hasn't.

"Barbizon appeals primarily to the lower-to-middle-income brackets, especially blacks and Hispanics, and it almost appears as if they do it deliberately, because—and this sounds very demeaning—those are usu-

At his request, Playgirl *shelved ex-boxer Jerry Gustin's nude photographs. Later, with his agency's approval, he posed for body studies. Photo: Ken Haak. A closer look at Gustin's face. Photo: Bruce Weber*

ally the people who won't call Ford or a big agency to see what their chances are. Barbizon benefits from that and treats minorities accordingly. The school attracts people who buy impulsively, whether it's a television set or a modeling course, and who don't really stop to think or investigate. There was one guy in the course who had held somebody up at gunpoint, and it was his second offense, and his parole officer said, 'You have a choice of going to jail or finding a school.' We were the school. He wasn't good-looking enough to make it as a male model, but he was there. His aunt borrowed money from her sister to send him.

"What happens a lot is, there'll be this really terrific-looking guy and because the school doesn't have any control over who enrolls, someone really exceptional will be thrown into, say, a Saturday class. Saturdays at Barbizon are total zoos. Every nerd in town, frankly, comes to Barbizon on Saturday. This one guy was thrown into a class of about eleven really not so wonderful-looking people, and he came to see me during a break and said, 'What is going on? It looks to me like a high-priced psychiatric session.' And I said, 'To be very honest with you, in many ways it is. But you have exceptional talent and I think you could be a very good model. The secret is to take the course very seriously, listen to every word, do everything the teachers suggest, because the teachers are very tuned into good-looking people.' Part of my job was to keep the guys who might have been losing interest or who had come to the realization of what was really happening from dropping out.

"I had another incident that made me really feel terrible. A pastor and his wife came in and enrolled their son. They made a down payment, signed on a Monday and their son was to start on Thursday. Wednesday, I got a call from this pastor, who said he had just got a hysterical call from his wife. She had been riding on the subway. This was just after a devastating story—mainly about the Barbizon Acting School—had appeared in *The Village Voice*. She had heard this discussion on trade and vocational schools and was so proud that they had just signed their son up for the course that she mentioned it to the people who were talking, and one of them said to her, 'Get him out *fast*.' So the pastor said to me, 'What's going on?' All I could say was, 'Sir, we have an active agency, it is working. If you and your wife would like to come in again, I'll be glad to give you a tour of the agency and show you our working people, show you tear sheets and all.' So I didn't lie to him, I didn't say, 'Oh, your son is fine,' or I didn't promise that his son would work. The pastor said to me, 'We're poor people. My wife is working to help us make ends meet. Six hundred and ninety-five dollars is a lot of money to us. But I'm very satisfied with your answers, and we'll start our son on Thursday.' So, I'd done my job. But I hung up with a very bad conscience. And, you see, I'd never seen the boy. Thursday, I saw him. A nice-looking boy, I thought. And then he smiled at me. He was all gums. His teeth receded up into his gums. He smiled at me with those gums and I thought, Aaaaagh.

"But I didn't lie. I didn't exaggerate. I didn't promise.

"I think the most unfortunate thing about schools is when they lead students to believe that they're going to be something they're not. If they would approach it from the standpoint of executive grooming or getting your act together, fine. But they know that the guy is there to be a *model*. And that's what they capitalize on. But they build a dream that rarely comes true. 'Do you know that a model can earn twenty thousand dollars a year on one national television commercial?' That's a standard line. They're not told that you can only do one commercial before you have to belong to SAG or AFTRA. They don't tell the guys that because that involves more money. Another standard line is, 'A catalog model can make up to sixty-five thousand dollars a year.' They're not saying *you* can do it. But that's what the dreamer hears. The guys in the ghettos, they're having a bad time at school, bad home situations, and they look at *GQ* and maybe they're even good-looking enough to model, maybe not, but all it takes is one person to light the spark, and they're off with it. That's part of the sales hype. A Barbizon graduate is guaranteed a place with the Barbizon agency. Forever.

"It's getting tougher and tougher in all states, because the states are cracking down. Schools must be licensed. And to be licensed, you have to have everything involved in your school approved by the state board of education. Now, many boards—I know in New York it's true—are very lax in following up to see that the schools are really doing what they're supposed to be doing. When I was with Barbizon, the interviewers worked on commission—maybe they still do—so if they didn't make a sale, they didn't eat the next week. They stress the fact that the schools are approved, which is supposed to mean something, and to the lower-income brackets, I suppose it would.

"I foresee a time within five years when there won't be any modeling schools, at least franchised ones. Because a school is only as good as its director. So many are franchised now. It's like a hamburger chain. You can eat at one franchise and have a good hamburger, or you can go two blocks down the street to another and have a rotten hamburger. Because some franchisees don't know anything about the business. I think that's true of most modeling schools. And there are complaints from disgruntled students, many complaints. The state laws are going to become much more stringent. Right now, because of the way the state laws are, it's more a matter of keeping your mouth shut. Interviewers are told not to talk potential, not to talk career, but to talk about the quality of the training, to get the guy to say, 'Yes, I'm the kind of person who goes through with what I commit myself to,' get a commitment and *money*. Get the guy to give fifty dollars, which is a commitment. Get him to sign the enrollment agreement, and you've got him.

"There's something else that could blow the whole business open. At Barbizon in New York, anyway, half of the people on the headsheet poster for fall 1978 were not even Barbizon graduates, though they are with the Barbizon agency. Let's suppose that you're John Doe, and you've just spent six hundred and ninety-five dollars for a Barbizon course, and you're on a go-see and right next to you is a guy who is also a Barbizon model, so the graduate says, 'Oh, you went to Barbizon?' and the other guy answers, 'Naw, I walked in off the street and they took me.' So, let's say to make the case even worse that the guy who's not the Barbizon graduate gets the job. Well, the guy who has just spent six hundred and ninety-five dollars is going to be a little upset.

"What kind of jobs do the graduates get? A few get some decent work—there are even a couple who get signed with big agencies—but mainly they get trade shows or conventions or they're asked to stand on street corners for five days passing out samples of True cigarettes."

Mary sighs and says, "I'd love to hear what the president of Barbizon would say to you. But I don't think he'll talk." Mary is correct.

Private modeling schools run by an individual owner are less likely to be the butt of negative reviews, but they don't receive blanket approval either. Schools associated with modeling agencies tend to be only as good as the agency, never better, sometimes worse. Whenever the school/agency is located in a city where the work load for male models is light, the quality of the school is frequently open to question. However, Jimmy Grimmé defends his school against the bad-mouthing most modeling schools receive by saying, "How can you possibly teach models how to be in front of a camera or how to show clothes on a ramp if you don't have an agency that constantly has models working? The look one season may be a very macho look, then maybe the slicked-back look, or the curly-haired look, the sloppy look. The look changes every season, so the model has to change with it. And how can a school make those changes if they have no agency? Another thing. If a guy comes in and is only five feet/seven, I'm going to tell him that he's too short, not to waste his time. Look, I don't even suggest to guys who come here hoping to be taken on by the agency that they take the classes. They have to bring it up. Even then, I'll never promise anyone we will take him in the agency after he completes the course, never. The course is open to anyone who wants to try to look like a model or act like a model or dress like a model. A lot of supposed prospective models come in saying they want to model because they don't really have the courage to say, 'Look, I want to advance in my job,' or whatever it may be. Maybe they're breaking up with a girl friend or a boy friend. A lot take the courses to help themselves, to give themselves more confidence. But they are never, never promised a place in the agency. After the course, the test shots are shown to me and I will say, 'No, no, no, no. Yes, let's talk to him. No, no, no, no.' But the guys are told the truth right from the outset."

Nothing is guaranteed if someone attends a modeling school. Neither is it if a fellow follows the suggestion of virtually every model agent:

Don't besiege an agency with letters and telephone calls; simply send a clear snapshot or two ("with a self-addressed envelope, please, dear God," moans Nina Blanchard) and wait patiently for a reply.

Lots of men, once the idea of modeling is sparked, charge agency doors. And are curtly turned away. A few agencies set aside one morning or afternoon a week for open calls—no appointments necessary; individuals are seen on a first-come, first-interviewed basis—but hopefuls will be seen only during those specified hours. A prospective model may wait for an hour or more only to undergo a less than five-minute examination that usually concludes with rejection. "Don't those guys own mirrors?" is the lament heard day after exasperated day in agencies around the country. By and large, the applicants are mediocre-looking ducklings who will never emerge as swans except in their hyperactive imaginations. "A salesman at Barney's tells a guy, 'Jesus, you look just like a model in that suit,'" jokes Joey Hunter, "and before you know it, he's up here with his prom pictures." Given the numbers of hopefuls who beleaguer them, most agency personnel do not dish out great dollops of compassion when out-and-out losers grace their waiting rooms. Having witnessed the greater cruelty of nurturing false hopes, they can be relentlessly honest in appraisals of too large noses, too short statures and pinched mouths. Not that they will gratuitously offer their harsher evaluations. Instead, the usual answer is, "I'm sorry, I just don't think that we have a place for you in our agency." But pressed for more specific reasons for rejection, the interviewers do not mince words, cutting many an ego in the process.

Inordinate numbers of men who by all objective standards haven't a prayer persist in believing their faces are their potential fortunes, and this exposes one of the many paradoxes of the profession. The self-deluding aspirants are prey to the same ambivalences concerning male models and modeling as is the country at large. On one level, male models are treated with contempt. Since they earn their livelihoods by selling themselves as visual commodities for the consumption of others, their profession is associated with the world's oldest. However, rather than being perceived as necessarily evil or wicked, male models are thought to be superficial, vain, neurotic and none-too-smart pretty boys, usually with a touch of lavender lurking in their souls. Yet, simultaneously, male models are considered glamorous and extraordinary; they literally stand out in any crowd. And since, as the consensus goes, they live off their God-given looks, not their brilliant intellects, models don't deserve a fraction of what they earn: theirs is not *honest* labor. The fallacy, of course, is that intellectual brilliance is also directly traceable to genetics, as is the physical stamina, strength and height of a basketball player. However, much of society resents models being given a free ride; it sees no true work associated with modeling. Because of this, many a male is simultaneously seduced and repulsed by the male model's world. "Damnit, why shouldn't I get a free ride, too?"

During junior high, Jim Gibbs fantasized about modeling but doubted he could make the grade.
Photo: Bill Farrell

Male models have the reputation of being extravagantly vain. But before taking their first tentative steps toward the career, many fellows are genuinely shocked when someone considers them model material.

Jim Gibbs, who spent a three-year stint as the Hathaway Man and who thinks his parents' "proudest moment" came when he was on the cover of Sears' Bicentennial catalog, says, "I never really thought I could model. I was probably in junior high school when I read an article in *Life* or *Look* on male models in New York and modeling sounded like a wonderful thing to do. For me, modeling as a career was just a dream. A couple times I worked myself up to go to an agency. I'd go to the front door, turn around and walk away. I didn't have the guts to open the door. Because I didn't think I was qualified physically to get in the front door. Later, a PR woman told me I should take a stab at modeling. All I needed was one person who knew anything about the business to say, 'Sure, you can do it.' I needed the encouragement. I always wanted to model; I never thought I could."

Conrad Bell, a fashion designer as well as a model, comes from Climax, Georgia. He recalls, "I would never ask anyone out for a date until I was in my third year of college because I thought I was so ugly and so skinny, so backward and awkward. Whenever people told me I was good-looking, I thought, What do they want? After I moved to California, I was having drinks and some guy who said he was an agent asked me if I would like to be an actor. Of course I wanted to be an actor, but I didn't want to say I wanted to be an actor at a bar next to an alcoholic old man who was telling me I would make a good actor. He was in such a blurred state, I could have had acne. I met him, sober,

Tony Stefano lacked confidence before heeding Skrebneski's advice.
Photo: Skrebneski

later, and he really was an agent, by the way. I think he had a great deal of respect for me because I had told him I didn't want to be an actor. Later, when people told me I should model, I went through the same mental routine: I always questioned what they wanted from me. Because I was so self-conscious about the way I looked."

Tony Stefano, one of the Eminence underwear models billboarded at bus stops around New York and other cities, credits a large measure

of his large success to photographer Victor Skrebneski. Stefano, comparing himself to the other "handsome devils" (as he calls them) in male modeling, says, "The only reason I was able to try to make a go of modeling is because of something Skrebneski said to me years ago—that it is not important to be good-looking; what is important is to have a good look. Otherwise, I would slink in a corner."

Self-conscious about their looks or not, most men have an unacknowledged quality lurking inside them—"vanity" is the word that comes closest to describing it—and it is quickly activated when they hear the magical words, "You should model." They may doubt that they can, but something—vanity?—makes them want to try, or at least believe they could model if they chose to. They want to believe they are physically desirable. To model would be the proof.

Les Hamaguchi, another of Victor Skrebneski's discoveries and the only male Oriental actively promoted by a major New York agency (Wilhelmina) from the mid-seventies onward, is far more honest than many when he candidly remarks, "Someone comes up to you and says,

'You're exotic looking' or 'You're interesting looking' or 'You can be an instant success,' that conjures up several things. It's flattering. It's an ego massage. I think people see modeling as being a mini-movie star. I certainly did. There's always the fantasy of seeing yourself as a model: people will be looking at *me*, and I'm one of the few men whose pictures are paraded across magazines. It's the whole thing of playing out the fantasy of being a star." Although Hamaguchi's primary source of income comes from being a senior account executive with a prestigious advertising agency, he has no pretenses about the ego boost modeling affords him.

Vanity can be healthy or it can be dangerous. The vain dreamer who lacks the physical attributes to model is in a very vulnerable position, not just emotionally but financially: in the periphery of the profession are some unscrupulous birds perched to swoop. Although agents constantly warn that no prospective model should pay for a group of professional photographs before being accepted, or at least encouraged by, a reputable agency, many unsuspecting guys believe their chances will improve if they approach an agency with a series of portraits. These men refuse to believe the words of Sharon Cooper, who presides over the A Plus Agency in Chicago, and who echoes the sentiments of every major agent in the nation: "I'd rather see a twenty-five-cent machine's strip photos from a dime store than have somebody go out and spend several hundred dollars for shots when the guy's never gonna work."

Jimmy Grimmé elaborates, walking animatedly around his office. "You'll get an unknown photographer who'll walk down the street and say, 'Hey, I like your looks. I'd like to shoot some pictures of you. Give me a hundred and fifty bucks.' And some guy will fall for it. I had one kid who came in here not too long ago. He'd never modeled. Without consulting me or an agency, he spent seven hundred and fifty dollars on his portfolio. I said, 'You're out of your mind.' Plus, they were shot by a portrait photographer who does nothing but weddings. A client would laugh his head off if I sent a guy to him with shots like that. He'd say, 'Grimmé has had another nervous breakdown.' That's why someone with aspirations should always find an agent first. And if an agent will not take him and he's still going to go out and pursue it, at least he'll get some advice as to what not to do."

A few aspirants, looking for exposure, end up literally exposing themselves. Some have no ambition other than to earn some extra dough by dropping their pants. Others believe that nude modeling can lead to a career as a "legitimate" model. Several successful models have indeed done nude print work in magazines, notably *Playgirl*, but as yet no top fashion model with any longevity has emerged from gay-oriented publications. Nevertheless, many beginners believe that doing nudes will help. If they are shot by a photographer who would otherwise refuse to photograph the beginner and he gets some portrait shots in the bargain, that's

According to industry jargon,
Les Hamaguchi is an "exotic."
Photo: Nancy Purser

possibly true. Otherwise, nude shootings may not hurt, but they never truly help the man who has the right material to begin with. A model with "the look" could get signed by an agency without having done skin work, but he might be refused by an agency if he has. As the head of one regional, medium-sized agency relates, "I had one very nice-looking black guy come in with a contact sheet full of pictures in fishnet underwear. I asked, 'Why did you do these?' And he answered, 'Well, the photographer told me that I had to have underwear shots, that all models have underwear shots.' And I said, 'You don't have to do nothing but die and pay taxes. And no one needs underwear or nude shots. Underwear advertising is a very exclusive part of modeling. If you're doing it professionally, you get paid double your rate, sometimes triple, and any underwear shots you see are airbrushed so the pubic hair is taken out. I don't know a male model who has underwear shots in his book.' And he said, 'Gee, I didn't know that.' "

Not all the guys are innocent victims. Since it is widely assumed that many male models are gay, it's not unusual for agencies to receive photographs that should arrive in brown wrappers. Instead, they come with notes expressing the sender's deep-seated desire to become a model. "We started a collection of all those horrible shots that are supposed to be sexual turn-ons—the too-nude, supermuscular ones or the super-starry-eyed types," muses Sharon Cooper, "but the file just got to be too big, so we decided to get rid of them. And then there were some shots so dreadful you couldn't believe them. Some ridiculous-looking people really think they're gorgeous. If they could really see themselves, it would be a bitter cup of coffee."

Experience indicates that a disproportionately large percentage of men who want to model are homosexual. The misconception that the whole field is rampantly gay may partially explain why so many gay men seize upon the notion of modeling. Ironically, because of the gay stereotype, homosexuals may actually find it harder to break into the business.

"Look, my agency is in San Francisco, which everybody knows has a large gay population," remarks Jimmy Grimmé. "So a lot of gay guys come to the city and some of them are very good-looking. It seems all of them want to be models immediately, maybe just thinking that they're going to walk into bars and get lucky very quickly. But I will not take a model if he is in any way obvious. I would say that the majority of the photographers and people in ad agencies are pretty straight. A guy can be the best-looking guy in the world, but have him come swishing in with a lisp and the whole bit, and they won't hire him. No way."

Michael O'Brien, a New York photographer known for shooting men's fashion, says, "I try to separate my knowledge of anybody's sexuality from the way that I know the person will photograph. I've had photographers say to me that they have used a certain model in a certain spread because that particular model was straight and because the client was very sensitive. But who the hell knows the difference? A picture is the way you construct the picture. Some of the most masculine-looking models are gay, and vice versa. I try to see how someone looks in a photo as opposed to what I know about him. Someone can be stupid but look very intellectual, or a guy can look very Continental but come from a small town in Tennessee. Who cares about someone's sex life? On the other hand, I do think that there is a prevalent attitude in gay society that modeling is some kind of pinnacle, so naturally I am called by more gay men than straight men who want to model, or so it seems. That doesn't speak well for gay society to lionize the profession. But there's this whole society—chic, well-tanned, summered—that some gay men seem to think is the pinnacle."

Since the model's work is illusion, the model's "real" persona is a side issue. (More about the psychological strain accompanying this phenomenon later.) Selfhood is self-evidently more complicated than sexual preference. However, the widespread premise is that male models must always appear in their work to be heterosexual, for in society's eye *maleness* is seen as exclusively heterosexual and overtly "masculine." (This one-dimensional view of maleness contributes to behavioral problems for many straight and gay men alike.) Since the male model deals in illusion, it is incumbent upon him to *appear* straight. So the male model's world is dimensioned by the closet, be the model gay or straight. Even though society may feel that homosexuality carries a stigma, model agencies do not, *not* because homosexuality is ubiquitous in modeling but because agencies are seeking that minuscule percentage of males, straight or gay, who can bring in the money and lots of it. Agencies don't want to make stars, they want to make profits, and they want only money-makers on their headsheets. Pragmatists first and foremost, agents will not sign up a flagrant queen but neither will they take on a guy hung up on his own macho, because both extremes are offensive to clients. Agents feel that a model's worth should be measured by how he performs before a camera, not by whom he performs with in bed. Nina Blanchard tries to laugh the question into perspective: "No guy is going to come into the male modeling field and be turned into a homosexual, for Christ's sake. It cracks me up when I hear that."

What qualifications must a man have for an agent to accept him? "A gut feeling that he's right, that he's got the look, that he'll make it," is the honest if vague answer that various agents express in various ways.

"It's not just being good-looking," analyzes Dan Deely who oversees Wilhelmina's men's division in New York, "and it's not just being photogenic. For want of a better word, there's some sort of magnetism that happens between the person's face and the camera that comes out on the printed page. I've known many people who are extremely handsome, beautiful, charming, whatever, who don't photograph well or haven't the personality to sell themselves. There must be something *special*. I hope, of course, that I can recognize it. That contributes to my success. But I can miss."

"You set a certain standard for the type of guy that you want," says Joey Hunter, "and also certain *types* that you want. That is, you might say to yourself, 'Well, this guy we have is successful so let's look for guys similar to him.' But that doesn't always work. Personality has a lot to do with it. Now, the person who's going to take on a new model has definite tastes. But we do have to work within the guidelines of what the advertisers will buy. Even though a model is my client, every time I look at a new guy I have to look at what my other client, the advertiser, wants and what fashion is dictating at the moment. There's no way if advertisers are hiring guys who look like they come from Oklahoma that I am going to go out and find guys who look like they come from Italy. What am I going to do with them? I don't consider myself a trend setter. I try to work within the guidelines of what I can sell. There are a few agencies in town that have tried to work against that by hiring really unique types. They get one or two big spreads and they don't really earn money. The key to the business is earning. I would say that the median income for guys who work reasonably often but are not superstars is between eighteen and twenty-five thousand dollars. If you can't earn that, you shouldn't be a model."

Although the popularity of different types—the Latin Lover, the California Surfer—may wax and wane from year to year, more rigid are size requirements. Ideally, the male fashion model should be 6 feet or 6 feet 1 inch tall. Under certain circumstances, he may be 5 feet 11 inches or possibly 6 feet 2 inches, but seldom shorter or taller. His suit size should be a 40 regular, although some fluctuation exists here as well. A shirt size of a 15- or 15½-inch neck and a 33- to 35-inch sleeve length, plus a 30- to 32-inch waist and a 31- to 34-inch inseam, are next to crucial. Admittedly, exceptions are made, but these are exceptions to exceptions, since the fellows encouraged by agencies to pursue the career are exceptions to begin with.

"It's so painful for me to look at a young man who is wonderful-looking but six feet/two and say, 'You're an inch too tall. You're really two inches too tall. It would be better if you were six feet. Or you could be five/eleven, five/eleven and a half, six feet, maybe six/one, but not six/two," says Kim Dawson, red hair framing her pale skin. "In Dallas, it's very precise. It seems to me that some of the better models in New York are smaller than guys in Dallas. Here, everybody just goes bananas if a model is one inch over or under the standard."

"Designers will make a suit sample to be photographed even before the clothes are manufactured," explains Dan Deely. "They don't just get a person and then get the size of the suit to fit the person. They already have the size. In this country, it's a forty regular. I don't know how they determined that, but that is what they determined. So that necessitates us getting men that size. You deviate too much from a forty regular and you're asking for trouble. A model may be the most fantastic-looking person in the world, but if he doesn't fit half the clothes, he can't work. There's no time I've ever known a designer to be so crazy about a model that the designer will change his sketches and make the sample to fit the model. Generally, it's better to be a bit smaller than larger. If you are a tiny bit smaller than the garment, it can be taken in. But only a tiny bit, not a great deal, because then the shape of the garment will be ruined. And a camera makes anyone look slightly larger and heavier, so if you have a big person to start off with, then the merchandise is going to look big and hulky."

"You don't want to be the one to say, 'No, you're never gonna make it,' because you're selfish," Nina Blanchard says of the agent's dilemma. "You don't want to feel like a shit again at the end of the day, you know? You've rejected somebody. No matter what the facts are, you've rejected a *person*. But I don't know what they expect of me, you know? And some guys get really hostile. They come in, and what do you say to a face full of pimples? Now, that angers me. A guy came in the other day and I didn't know how to deal with him. The guy's a deaf-mute. Now, how am I going to deal with that? A girl came in with one leg. Now, Jesus, I hate to sound cruel, but ours is a profession of beauty. Sure, she can go be an actress. He could maybe go work in the deaf theater, but what the Christ am I going to do with them? 'Well, can't I just do pictures where they show me from the waist up?' says the girl with the one leg. 'Or I could sit down all the time.' Jesus. I don't like to be played games with, and when people do that to me, it angers me. Because they have no respect for the business and haven't even tried to learn anything about it. I have a high regard for our business and the professionals in it. I wish the guy who's a deaf-mute all the luck in the world. And maybe in modeling he would not be impossible. It would be hard. He could read lips. I would say, probably, someone who's a deaf-mute if he were attractive would stand a better chance in our business than someone who had pimples. But people have to face the fact that this is a business with requirements. The guy who comes in and gets nasty with me because he's five/eight and I can't do anything with him, he gets me furious. All guys like that are dealing with is a fantasy of being famous, which I also understand, but our business has physical requirements, damnit."

Most fellows, told they lack the physical requirements, resentfully give up. Michael Slaven didn't. Despite his 37 regular suit size, he modeled professionally in Kansas City, Missouri, before tackling the big time.

"In Kansas City I worked quite often for Hallmark Cards and at a huge shopping center that did fashion shows every day. I did sometimes two shows a day. I was also doing ads for Macy's and catalogs for Macy's and another local store, earning twenty-five dollars an hour. But after a year of that, I'd done everything there was and I was really overexposed. So I figured, I'll just sweep New York.

"I called the modeling agencies and the first time around, I was able

Michael Slaven
Photo: Donald Kennedy

to get in everywhere except at Wilhelmina, because I gave them my long list of credits from Kansas City. When they saw me, they asked, 'What size jacket do you wear?' Zoli told me I had a terrific look, but I should go back to Kansas City. But I kept plugging away. I kept testing for a whole year.

"I think a lot of times the reason I stuck with it is because of my family and my friends back in Kansas. I was the only person to leave. The first year and a half, the only time I called home or called my friends was after I'd get a job."

Eventually Slaven signed with an agency that specialized in commercial, not fashion, models. His feet, hands and stomach were photographed, but he did not do a fashion shooting until he presented himself at Saks Fifth Avenue with his portfolio. He had done test shots with a photographer who was doing work with Saks, and that made the difference. Slaven was given three fashion bookings. "As soon as those pictures came out, I called all the agencies again. I was sure I was on my way this time. It was the same old thing. They said, 'Yeah, you did get the Saks thing. But we make money from models doing shootings before the garment goes on the rack, from size forty models.' "

A Parisian agency sent a scout to New York to recruit models for its newly formed men's division. The scout saw Slaven's photographs and was impressed. Since he was off to Europe for a vacation, Slaven agreed to make a side trip for an interview in Paris. "When I went in, they really liked me and they said they thought they could pull it through even though I really was too small for Europe even. So I said, 'Well, I'm willing to give it a try.'

"I always made enough money to pay the rent and get a little food, but the thing was, I was actually working as a full-time model. For the first time in my life. Because everywhere else I had to wait tables and all that. Still, almost every interview I went to, they liked my pictures and I'd put on the jacket and it would just hang over my shoulders. They'd say, 'Well, maybe we can use you for photography but not for runway.' "

Slaven sent out composites to agencies in Germany (the highest-paying modeling center in Europe) and Italy. He was rejected by all the German agencies. "I got a telephone call from Milan saying, 'We want you as soon as you can come down.' So I took off. But I didn't work very much. The clients would say, 'This is what we're shooting, why don't you try it on,' and as soon as I did that, the job was lost. There are tricks, like filling up your chest with air or bending your arms, but as soon as you move, so much for that. In Paris, I had finally given in and bought lifts. That makes you tall enough, but that still doesn't make a jacket or pants fit. Anyway, I left Milan.

"When I got back to Paris, I decided officially, okay, I've done it. It's time to go back home. I was living on a shoestring. My agency in Paris had shown my pictures to Elite in New York. They really liked my pictures, so I felt that I had to go by at least and, if they were interested, sure, why not. We got along fine. But then they said, 'Would you consider buying one of those vests to wear under the jacket to pull you almost up to a forty regular to make the jacket fit? And would you wear lifts?'

"The funny thing, I had my lifts on that day when I went to the interview. I was wearing my cowboy boots to make me look taller, plus lifts to make me taller, and they were asking if I would consider wearing lifts and wearing this vest. I thought it was really hilarious. And that's when I said to myself, I don't really feel like remaking my whole body. I like me the way I am. For once it was, 'Well, I'll think about it and *I'll* call *you*.'

"A couple of days later I decided I'd get on with other things." Today, Slaven is doing television and commercial work, his career as a sometime fashion model over.

Modeling is an irrational business. During the starting-out days, every hope the would-be model has (prior to receiving official endorsement) is challenged by reality. Some—the fewest of the few—will indeed become proverbial overnight successes. Most will discover that the first days and months are arduous and humiliating, that modeling ain't what they had thought. Although a model's life revolves around illusion, illusions are shed more rapidly than inhibitions at a New Year's Eve party, without the merriment.

*Renauld White
waits backstage
for a runway show to
begin. Photo: Peter Sakas*

starting out

The navy was wonderful for me. I didn't want to stay in school and study for a degree when I knew all I wanted was to act. So I left. I joined the navy just to clear it with the folks, with girl friends, with everything. I just wanted to leave the scene.

I grew up in the navy. I woke up to a lot of realities and a lot of discipline. I was twenty-two when I got out. I was in Florida and I liked it, so I got a job at a radio station in Daytona Beach writing copy, which was amazing since I'd never written anything. And keeping the books. I got involved right away in little theater. I was doing plays at night and working at the radio station during the day and having a wonderful life.

Through one of the plays, a woman I was working with suggested I might like to do summer stock in a professional company. She wrote the director and I got the job. In Tamworth, New Hampshire. My first professional acting job. After the summer was over, I returned to Florida. I played the lead in *The Drunkard* for six months in Miami Beach. One of the members of the cast was doing commercials and said I should too. I met Ann Wright, an agent. I went in with my old pictures and she said I needed some new ones, which I got. They were no better than the old pictures, but instantly I got three Polaroid commercials.

I had the checks sent home because I was moving around from place to place. I called my mother and asked, "Do I have any money in the bank?" She coughed a few times before saying, "Yes." So I asked, "How much?" and she coughed some more and answered,

"I'm not sure you want to know." I was beginning to worry about
her throat. "Yes, I do," I said, and she said, very quietly,
"About twenty thousand dollars. I'm afraid you're going to spend it."
Which I promptly did.

I decided it was time for me to travel. I just played.
Spent it on anything I wanted. Play. Travel. I moved back to L.A.

I thought I could do commercials there as well. And I did, lots
of them. It was a good living. I did some TV things, like *Bewitched*.
I'd also acted in the *Gentle Ben* series while I was in Florida.
I skated in the roller derby, and did some theater, *The Dirtiest Show in
Town*, in and out of clothes. I was also in a singing group for a year.
I did a lot of things in L.A. Then I went to New York on a
vacation. A friend—a model—suggested I meet his agent. The
agent was Tom Hahn. He was opening up a men's division for Stone.
We met socially and he asked me if I was interested in modeling.
I said no, because I wasn't. I didn't think it was a career for me.
I had a career in commercials. Then he asked, "If you left a picture
and I put it on my headsheet and I got you work, would you come
back to do it?" It wouldn't cost me a penny. I had brought my pictures
with me because I had intended to see commercial agents while I
was in New York, which in fact I did. In L.A., I'd had other pictures
done by a very good commercial photographer. I gave Tom one of

After the navy, Taylor acted in summer stock. A publicity
still from Tiger at the Gate *(left). He also did TV*
commercials in Miami. A photograph from his commercial
composite, 1968 (right).

those pictures. Very smiley, very up. And I dismissed the idea.

I still thought of models as very perfect people. Perfect physical specimens. I wasn't that. I was a real person and an actor. I certainly didn't think I qualified to be on the pages of a magazine representing some sort of ideal.

I was told that I was good-looking and I was with attractive people as mates, so I knew I wasn't bad-looking. But when I looked in the mirror, I wasn't enthralled, I wasn't captivated by my own looks. Truthfully, I was insecure about them. I always thought that people were attracted to my personality, not my looks. I would look out at the world and see people whom I thought were extremely good-looking and they didn't look like me. I was thrilled that Tom thought that someone might want to hire me as a model. But I thought he was wrong. I got on the plane and flew back to L.A.

Tom called a week later to say that he had sent my picture to *GQ* and they wanted to use me for a six-day trip to the Bahamas. Was I interested? *Was* I interested? I was flattered, thrilled at the prospect. I wasn't quite sure what *GQ* was, but I knew it was a men's fashion magazine and I thought, God, they want to take me to the Bahamas for six days and pay me!

Then I found out I had to send more pictures. It was only a *tentative* booking. They wanted me to send more photographs. They wanted to see what, in fact, my body was like. I did have

"I thought, God, this is fabulous, this is a knock-out business," says Taylor of his first modeling assignment, a six-day trip to the Caribbean for the winter 72/73 issue of GQ. Photo: Jacques Malignon. Courtesy of GQ.

a swimsuit shot, which I sent with a couple other shots.
I got the booking.

I flew to New York for a fitting. The job was ten pages for the winter
72/73 issue. Summer wear, bathing suits and light suits and all that.
Harry Coulianos was art director then too. And Brian Burdine
was also there at that time. So off we flew to the Bahamas.
With the fashion editor, who was out to lunch. The photographer.
A girl, a Cuban girl who has since left the business. Beautiful.
And, of course, Brian and Harry.

The shooting was fine. I wasn't sure if I was doing the right things
at times, but I assumed they would tell me if I wasn't.

We stayed on houseboats on an island called Eleuthera.
Each of us had our individual houseboat. We ate at the restaurant,
anything we wanted. Lobsters and shrimps and all the wine.
When we weren't shooting, we were lying in the hot, hot sun
putting oil over our bodies. We'd do a shot here, a shot there,
and I thought, God, this is fabulous, this is a knockout business.

Right then and there I decided on modeling as a career. Being
paid $350 a week for this was icing. Hell, I thought, I'll go for it. I can
do this as well as act. Look, my first job was for the top men's fashion
magazine in the country. I thought the rest would just fall
into place. Sunning myself on that white sand, I decided to move
to New York because that was where the modeling action was.

I didn't like New York at first. It wasn't the same. I'd been spoiled
by the Bahamas. I'd been whisked via limousine to be whisked away
on a jet. I'd lived on a houseboat. I was whisked away by another
limousine to another jet. And then I was dumped onto the streets
of New York. It was filthy. It was crowded. I didn't have the
money to get an apartment. I stayed with friends. When I checked into
the agency, they said, "Now, here's a rounds list."

I felt as if I had duped myself. I'd allowed myself to believe
New York was waiting with open arms to embrace me, to take me
to every port in the world to be photographed by every camera in the
world. No one was waiting, except me. It would be three more months
before my issue of *GQ* came out. I didn't even have pictures to
prove I'd done the job in the Bahamas.

I talked to Tom, who said, "I think you'll be an excellent model.
You're too tall to get some work. Some catalogs won't hire you
because you're six/three, but you've had an excellent beginning. What
you have to do now is go out and meet all the photographers and all
the ad agents, to get your career going." I had thought my career

This picture was taken as a publicity shot for
commercial work in L.A., but Taylor also used it in
1971 on his first composite for Stone in New York.

was going just great, when it hadn't even started. I had no pictures
except my commercial portfolio. Tom said I'd have to test.
Great. It's great to test if you have clothes to test in. I had boots,
Levis and some shirts, plus a scruffy jacket. I had to learn a fashion
sense. It was at that point of bow ties and sweater vests and
plaid pants and little round shoes with high heels. Those clothes
had nothing to do with Michael Taylor. I could borrow them from
GQ, but I felt awkward and ill at ease.

Tom not only gave me a list of photographers, he made
appointments for me daily. And he made sure I went to them.
I have a tendency to be lazy when there's no pot of gold highly
visible at the end of the rainbow. I didn't see any immediate results,
so I avoided some of the rounds. Tom was great in that he got on
my ass and said, "You *go*. Go, you work. Don't go, you don't work."
So I went. Resenting it. My bubble had burst.

My first test was with one of this country's—the world's—
biggest photographers. A friend had set it up for me. I met the
photographer. It was rather apparent he had other thoughts in mind
besides photographing me. He had other designs. So I decided to
use that. I thought, Why not pretend interest, then grab the photos
and run? Clever little devil that I was. He was very, very successful,
and I wanted his photos. So I played him. Jesus, I really did.
And he bought it. I used it. To get the pictures. I borrowed a suit
from *GQ* and went to his studio for my test. He photographed
me but I didn't deliver. I didn't pay up. And I never got those
photographs—there was nothing to run with. People find out your
game real fast, and if you don't pay, they don't pay. So I ended up
with no pictures and he ended up with no nookie.

—M.T.

With visions of cigarette ads dancing in their heads, most newly
registered male models believe they can recline in their armchairs while
their agency propels them inexorably to stardom. Wrong.

"Most guys usually don't make it because they aren't that interested,"
says Nina Blanchard. "They think modeling is a hobby. And they treat
it as a hobby. They don't understand it's a profession. And they're god-
damned lazy."

As Tom Hahn, vice president of Mary Webb Davis, another Los Angeles agency, remarks, "An agent can only do so much by putting out a

headsheet, making sure the model's composite is sent out. Then it's up to the model to get around and see clients. And if the fellow doesn't follow through on that side with personal appearances, the client's not going to be aware of him, and jobs will be very slow coming in."

Many of the new guys don't even know what a headsheet or a composite is. An agent's approval doesn't automatically transform them into models, as they may imagine: that approval merely makes them apprentices who can learn their craft through on-the-job training. Before mastering a new vocabulary, however, the greenhorn model first learns about arithmetic.

In New York City, the highest-paying center for modeling, a starting-off model may earn $60 or $75 an hour, not the highly-touted $100 that veterans or hot properties can command. And 15 to 20 percent of that fee will be paid in commission to the agency. (The agency also charges a 10 percent service charge to the client.) On a 20 percent arrangement, the model's total weekly earnings, minus commission, are paid him at the end of the week. However, under a 15 percent agreement, the models must either wait for payment until the client has paid for his services (which can sometimes take up to six months), or else the model is paid only a portion of the fee with the remainder held in reserve until the client coughs up the whole thing. But the hourly fee is not always firm. For example, a special editorial rate exists on fashion magazine shootings for the likes of *Gentlemen's Quarterly*: that rate is a big $125 a day (as opposed to $600 to $750 for standard bookings) and the commission remains the same. Even less heartening, an agent may decide that a new model must first get together a portfolio (sometimes called a book) before he can be seen by paying clients. In the meanwhile, the new model must go through a process called testing. The glowing star on the horizon can dim with frustration.

Although specific details vary for each beginning model, almost everyone goes through roughly the following routine. First, he is accepted by an agency. That acceptance may be as tenuous as "Yes, we'd like to represent you, but first you must bring us more photographs to work with," or as concrete as "Sign your name on the dotted line." Depending upon the city, the agent may demand that the model be exclusive with that agency, a standard practice in most major markets. Surprisingly, not all agencies require formal written contracts. Zoli Men in New York is one that does not.

"Models' contracts are legally binding, but, in a sense, they're not," remarks Zoli, a soft-spoken, diffident man. "If models can't get out of their contracts, they'll simply refuse to show up on their jobs. If a model isn't happy, I would never try to keep him here because life at the agency would be too difficult. This business is founded on close relationships. It's very personal. If someone isn't happy, what does it matter what's down on a piece of paper?"

Jeff Rowland, after losing the ten pounds Dan Deely, his agent at Wilhelmina, told him to drop. Photo: Ken Haak

Once contractually signed or informally taken aboard, the prospective model customarily discovers that his agent wants to change something about the very appearance that he thought was his meal ticket.

"I came here from Ohio, where I had done a little work," recounts Jeff Rowland, a relative newcomer to New York modeling. "I came up with three pictures. I had a contact at Ford but I decided to check out Wilhelmina too. So I went there weighing one seventy, which I thought looked nice. Dan Deely told me he liked my look and everything but I still had a lot of baby fat on my face. 'You have to lose ten pounds. And you have to cut your hair.' I knew I'd have to cut my hair, but I thought it would be smart to leave it long until I was told how short it should be. So I did that. This was on a Wednesday. Not by the following Monday, but the one after that, I had lost ten pounds. I drank orange juice blended with a raw egg in the morning. And then I had an apple for supper and that's all I ate—honestly, that's all I ate. I just killed myself. I was so weak, but I thought that once I lost the ten pounds, I could maintain my weight. I thought I could go back to eating whatever I wanted. Which is not true. I love sweets. I could eat a bag of M&Ms a day. I only eat one meal a day now. But I drink a two-liter bottle of Tab and half of another one each day. So I drink three liters of Tab a day, and I can just imagine what my insides look like."

Denis La Marsh, sometimes called "The Beard" by friends, has a special look that has paid off well; he is a highly visible and a highly paid model on the New York scene. "A friend of mine who had been 'discovered' by Ted Dawson—Ted had an agency at that point—took me to see him and Ted looked at me and said, 'Yes, I'd like to put you on the headsheet.' It was a total shock, because at that time I was into the hippie thing. I had the biggest beard ever, down to my chest, and hair to my shoulders. I had dropped out and I wasn't working and I had enough money to live on and I was just kind of breezing along. And I said, 'Well, all right, just for a gas, for a kick, but I will not cut my hair or my beard.' Ted was very, very patient. And just persevered with me till I got it together. He kind of kept saying, 'I want you to look like a country gentleman.' He absolutely had a look for me in his mind right away. But I was basically resistant. It took me eight to nine months before I cut the hair. Finally I did it; my money ran out and I needed some money. As soon as I got myself looking right, it started to happen. But I didn't really start making money for another eight months."

Jimmy Grimmé believes, "Models have to know their good points and their bad points. If you can't hide the bad points, then take advantage of them. I have a model in the agency with a very long chin. So I'm playing it up. There's no way to chop off his chin, and he's a good model. Artificially, with makeup, we put a cleft in the chin to draw attention to it. And he has his eyelashes dyed. So now the first thing you see in a photograph is great eyes and the cleft on the chin. It is not an effeminate thing to do; it's a smart thing to do."

Bruce Bauer, recognizable to many television viewers because of the numerous commercials he has done, remarks, "When an agent tells somebody to lose ten pounds or to get a haircut, that doesn't mean the guy is fat or has terrible hair. It means that the agent knows what sells. If you don't want to lose weight or get a haircut, then fine. Don't try to model. As models, we have to do whatever has to be done to get better photos. We are our own product. When I look in a mirror when I'm working, I want to make sure the product is right. Our looks are tools of the trade. If you want to be an engineer, you don't walk in knowing nothing about engineering and say, 'Hi, I'm here, give me a ruler.' Well, someone can't just say, 'Hey, I'm good-looking, give me a modeling contract.' This is bullshit. There are things to learn. And making the most of yourself is one of the things to learn."

Once physical alterations have been tended to, the newcomer is told to assemble a range of photographs, a task more easily advised by the agency than accomplished by the man. This is the testing period. The agency supplies the hopeful with a list of photographers who test. The basis of the procedure is that photographers are testing new equipment, new film, new techniques or new ideas, and the model is a guinea pig: the model offers his services without charge in order to work with professional photographers to gain confidence in his craft and ultimately to obtain good photographs.

In New York, models with established agencies seldom pay for test photographs, although they may have to absorb film and/or printing costs. In other cities, particularly San Francisco, some models are expected to pay $100 or more for the honor of testing. This is an inequity, say some models and agents, because the photographer uses the pictures for his portfolio.

"When I started out, I had to pay," relates Ruben Warfield with the Grimmé agency in San Francisco. "I put my book together and then went out looking for jobs. All I got was three or four jobs, and then there were five months of starvation. I redid my book and had to pay again. I just persisted, kept seeing photographers, kept hounding clients, ran there and there. Now that I'm working, and I have a lot of pictures in my book, photographers will look at it and say, 'Well, do you wanna test?' Mine is a face that's been in the paper recently and it's coming up a lot, and photographers have to see clients who might say, 'Okay, we used Warfield last time for an ad and that was good, and you know how to work with him,' so that will help the photographers get work. But now I'm not paying for any testing."

Nearly all novice photographers test with models, but when photographers become established, the frequency of their testing drops drastically. For one thing, their time becomes more valuable. For another, most photographers who have reached a plateau of relative success have a coterie of models with whom they enjoy working. It's no easy task for a new model to enter that charmed circle. Proven photographers may look for new faces but they spend less effort to uncover them.

Most often the novice simply feels rejected. Don Guide explains, "I just started pounding the pavement, which was a real thing, it was tough, you know. Twenty people a day. And out of twenty, ten weren't in. And of the ten that were, about seven of them didn't even want to waste their time looking at a male model. With women I had a better chance of getting in. I walked into one studio and saw this photographer

playing Ping-Pong. I'd never been introduced to him, but I knew who he was. I saw him playing Ping-Pong, and a secretary came out saying, 'He's busy just now.' A knife in my heart. I mean, I was standing there just trying to make a living and to establish myself. There are some real letdowns when people brush you off like that."

Not *every* photographer is a purposeful impediment to the aspiring model's career, but to most beginners it surely seems that *most* are. There are arrogant photographers who treat models "like a piece of meat," a phrase widely used by models to describe the cold indifference encountered during their early days, and often their later ones, too.

Nonetheless, photographs are essential, which means that the indignities associated with testing must be endured. By now the fledgling model comprehends the true worth of photographs. They serve in much the same capacity as a resumé does for someone in another profession. Pictures are credentials; a model needs photographs to prove his worth. It has been battered into his head that prospective clients will ask to see his book or portfolio. Literally, this is nothing more than a binder that holds his photographs and tear sheets (pictures torn from a magazine, newspaper or catalog to document work the model has done if he's fortunate enough to have done any). Symbolically, his portfolio is his claim to fame and identity. Without one, he probably won't even get inside a prospective client's door. In fact, now he understands that he must have a whole variety of pictures and looks for his book, since a successful model is a versatile one. He'll need a good head shot—a portrait focused on the face and very little else. And he should have a body shot, though it should not be a nude and need not be in a bathing suit; a bare chest (or one exposed in a tight T-shirt), clinging jeans and a smile (or a frown) can complete the costuming. And he should have a photo in a business suit. Plus a sports shot. Plus a boy-girl shot. Plus a mood shot. Plus a high-fashion shot. Plus . . .

Time for another zinger. He needs clothes. His jeans and cowboy boots won't pass for a conservative businessman's attire. Nor will a three-year-old blazer: if he's to look fashionable, he should be seen in a jacket sporting this year's lapel width. And by now he's heard that models are often expected to supply all or at least part of their wardrobe for certain shootings. Maybe he's lucky enough to borrow the necessary outfits for tests, but eventually he'll have to own his own wardrobe.

What has he gotten himself into? Well, a career with fewer rookies than there were yesterday, because a whole group of guys has already called it quits. But they'll be replaced by a new crop tomorrow.

The diligent neophyte is worried about another factor. He has to get together a card, but preferably a composite. A card is usually a two-sided 6″ x 8″ compilation of photographs—one side generally with a head shot, the other usually with no more than three photographs of

Ruben Warfield found testing in San Francisco difficult—and costly. Photo: Jamison Goodman

Body shot of Tony Stefano. Photo: Skrebneski. Rob Yoh's composite cover. Photo: Arthur Elgort. Two pages of the headsheet brochure for Zoli Men.

ROB YOH

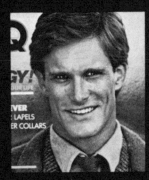

GREG HENRY
6' 40R 15½-34 10 $100
S.A.G. A.F.T.R.A.

MICHAEL HOLDER
6' 40R 15½-34 9½ $100

JOHN HOFFMEISTER
5'11½'' 39-40R 15-34 9 $100
S.A.G. A.F.T.R.A.

KELLEY JACKSON
6' 40R 15½-33 9½D $100
S.A.G.

PETER JAEGER
6'1'' 40R/L 15½-34 11D $100
S.A.G.

HUNTER JOHNSTON
6'1'' 40R/L 15½-34 10E $75

JOOP
6' 40R 15½-34 9½ $100
S.A.G.

PAUL KECKONEN
6' 39R 15½-35 9½ $75

TONY LAGO
6'1'' 40R 15½-34 10 $100

differing types—that also lists the model's name, measurements and agency affiliation. A composite is a more elaborate affair, either 6″ x 8″ or 8½″ x 11″, consisting of four to six sides—the front usually a head shot, an assortment of other pictures on the remaining sides— plus name, statistics and affiliation. Cards and composites are printed in large quantities because they are left with photographers and clients just as an executive drops off his business card as a tangible reminder of who he is and what he does. A moderate run of black-and-white cards costs about $800, an all-color composite up to $3,000 or more, and models, even the fledglings, must fork out the cash from their own pockets. They also shell out the mailing costs involved in sending cards or composites to the agency's list of clients.

Then there's the agency headsheet. It can be either a booklet or a poster containing head shots of each of the agency's models along with their sizes and rates. If a model isn't on it, he can easily be overlooked in the competitive marketplace. And does the agency pay for the production of the headsheet? Not entirely. Agencies say that the cost to models is "nominal." Well, one such nominal cost, when one new agency began in the mid-1970s with brash hoopla and an extravagant booklet, was $800 to each model. A more sedate headsheet for another men's division cost each model pictured $70, although the agency says that *its* cost per model was $200.

Every aspect of the business reinforces the pressure for the beginning model to push himself to do test after test after test, even though the opportunities to do so are severely limited. Furthermore, the beginning model is often hypersensitive to real or imagined threats. Even the men who claim that they have never felt a need to defend their maleness, when asked what they would change about male modeling, mention without exception they would like to erase the gay connotation to the business. Also high on that list of what to stamp out are the pervasive notions that male models are stupid and that they are shallow.

So the rookie who once thought that he could treat modeling as a lark starts experiencing full-force the personal strain that accompanies society's stereotyping of him. Even the blind hero worship he receives in some quarters seems hollow because it *is* blind. He tries to laugh off the situation or rationalize it away, but inside he smarts. Yet he is in the position that he must charge ahead with as much energy as he can muster to get his book, his composite and his head together. He faces rejection from inside the business as well as outside. To anchor himself, he concentrates on monetary rewards. Doing so can compound his insecurity because those rewards are out of his grasp until he gets himself rolling, something he can't do without a selling book and a solid composite, and something he can't do with a negative attitude or a chip on his shoulder. Given this strain, he often takes irrational refuge in hiding the fact that he is a model. Well over half the men who enter the field have pretended they belong to other professions. Patrick McElroy, a

Patrick McElroy hid the fact that he modeled for a year. Photo: Jean Ann Bybee

Dallas model, tells a story that is more exaggerated than most but one that captures the essence of how many guys have felt:

"Modeling is not a conventional job. It almost seems to be a little world that functions with the rest of the world on another frequency. The first couple months I was frustrated, extremely frustrated. It was as though the agency had given me a set of instructions but that someone had torn off the last three lines. Where was the bottom of the page? I thought I was doing everything except the last three lines, because nothing was working. That goes back to attitude. I like the hell out of modeling now. I would never say I was ashamed of it at all, but it was the sort of thing I thought would be difficult to explain, my being a model, so I just didn't bother. I just didn't say anything about it until the obvious part, when someone I know very well said, 'That looks like *my* kid. What is he doing in the newspaper with someone else's clothes on?' Then began a flood of explaining. And it was a *flood*. I had managed to pull it off a year. It was a lot of mumbling and excuses. I used to disappear from a lot of places when I had jobs. I didn't lie about it; it just seemed such a nuisance to explain. Everyone has preconceived notions about models. And I knew that the people I knew wouldn't understand my wanting to be a professional model, that if I were a professional model then I would no longer be Patrick McElroy, like some type of metamorphosis would take place. And, sure enough, that was the initial reaction."

On the other hand, certain beginning models mentally polish the stardom aspects of the career to rebuild their flagging confidence. They fabricate an elaborate sense of personal displacement by saying, "If I am rejected, I must remember that it is not *me* that's being rejected. It's just that I don't happen to be the type of person the photographer is looking for. He may not want this *image* of me, but someone else will. Either way, *I* am not involved, only an image of me is." The rationalization sounds good. The problem is the model feels personally rejected anyway, despite all the double-talking he's subjected himself to. His mental pep talks don't spare him subconscious feelings of inadequacy. Even "overnight successes" are never instant enough, not after the moment has passed and a new day dawns.

The unpredictability of the business may feed certain fellows hope initially, but it is also always a potential source of depression. While the novice is making the rounds to create a portfolio, he takes the contact sheets from the test shootings (when he's fortunate enough to obtain them) to his agency. There, more than likely a disagreement ensues over his image of himself versus the image the agency believes he should project or capitalize on.

"The first pictures somehow always look as if the guy is faking it, trying to live up to his preconceptions of how a model should look," analyzes Nina Blanchard. "Right now, frequently they're too brooding, because guys pattern themselves after their favorite models. Of course, it doesn't work. I have met probably three models in my lifetime that I would trust to choose their own pictures from a testing. The most common mistake is they want to look too unique. They want to get away from the commercial image. But it's the goddamn commercial image that sells them. And we fight tooth and nail."

The model who wants to see himself as extraordinary is shot down and told not to be. Yet photographers usually don't want to do test shots with ordinary models in ordinary situations. Testing is an experiment, an attempt to create some extraordinary illusion. Meanwhile, the arguments continue within the agency walls about what pictures to place in the portfolio and which ones not. Tempers may be flaring by the time the composite is being designed and a photo for the headsheet is being selected. Most often the model loses.

Joey Hunter opts for the voice of reason and of experience—his own. "A model's image of himself may not be selling at the moment. So I have to have some say about what I feel will make him sell. He likes this picture and I don't. 'It's my worst look,' he says of my choice, 'it's too commercial.' But that's the whole point, making the model commercial enough to sell. You get somebody who's twenty-two and wants to look like Ted Dawson. So he keeps on taking Ted Dawson pictures, Ted Dawson poses. It makes no sense. Why compete against Ted Dawson? Ted Dawson doesn't have to work at looking like Ted Dawson, he *is* Ted Dawson. The big thing for a model is to look the way he himself looks. I can't say often enough, 'This is you and this is the way you'll be walking around all day. Have different looks in your book, but for your head shot, I want you looking just as you look when you walk inside a client's door.' "

With his compromise composite under his arm, the model now has his business card and is ready to look for work in earnest. While his agency is telephoning its client list to hype him up, he's scurrying about (or should be) making himself known.

"You go through a lot of crap in the beginning," admits Tom Hahn, telephones constantly ringing, models coming and going. "That's why if you don't believe in yourself to begin with, you're never going to get there because you don't gain that much confidence in the beginning.

The first six months to a year are the hardest part in male modeling. Why does somebody want to be a male model? Besides the obvious reason that everybody says, that they like the money? Unless they're honest enough to say that they want the attention, they're never going to be good. It all boils down to that kind of a thing. You want to be recognized. And you want approval. It's that simple."

And the model wants bookings as well. A booking is simply another word for a job. However, a model never arranges his own bookings. A booker at the agency negotiates fees and takes down all the information about time, place, wardrobe and any other special instructions. These jobs are noted on a chart for each model. Also chronicled are go-sees, which are somewhat like auditions in that a client (whoever ultimately books the model, be that person a photographer, designer, advertiser, manufacturer, magazine editor, whoever) has asked to see a specific model or a particular type of model for a future job. Cattle calls are go-sees gone amok, when everyone and his uncle is being seen. General appointments are set up by the agency staff so that a model can introduce himself to a prospective client even though the client may not be casting a job at that precise time. Should the model get booked, after completing the job he fills out a voucher with the date and time worked, amount charged and assorted data for the client to sign; retaining one copy himself, the model gives two copies to the agency for billing.

Once the beginning model thought that the only real modeling was magazine covers or billboards. Now he knows that the work is much more varied and that to maximize his earnings he should try his face at each and every type of job.

Editorial work—the idea of which previously filled his nostrils with the scent of greenbacks—may still offer the most personal gratification because posing in fashion magazine layouts is prestigious and often includes location shootings. But editorial work has its price—the lowest one a model earns. But the investment can pay off big.

Runway work is modeling clothes on a ramp or stage in a fashion show. But in Eddie Davis' case, one of his first runway appearances was in a state of undress usually considered unfashionable. It was during a show at the Dallas Apparel Mart. "The idea was that everyone was going on this trip, a pleasure cruise. I was the chauffeur. In the first scene I came out with the bags and I went down the runway and the girls came out and did their things. The next scene was on the island. And I had to wear this—well, I don't know what you would call it, but to me it looked like a diaper. I was standing out there with my arms crossed and my legs spread, and these girls were walking around me and I said, 'Oh, my God.' My legs were shaking. I thought I was going to throw up. But the whole experience was weird. I remember arriving before the show. I walked into the dressing room—they have these double doors—and just pushed this door and saw all these naked bodies. I said, 'Oh, my God. I am in the wrong place.' But I wasn't. And

I thought, Why didn't they tell me I would have to change with all these naked girls? You don't want to stare, but . . ."

Few men are indifferent to runway work. In many cities the runway rate is lower than the standard print fee. Often there is little or no time for rehearsal. The positive side is the sense of immediacy the presence of an audience imparts. Conrad Bell, whose most prized modeling experience was being photographed in his own fur collection on location for Neiman-Marcus in Russia, attributes his success as a model to runway exposure. "See, I was always good on the runway, and Calvin Klein and Ralph Lauren and some of the other top designers started using me on the runway even though I wasn't being used at all for print work. But on the runway I had a certain style that separated me from everyone else, I think. It was that I didn't know how to walk. I really didn't know what to do, except that I would discover what was interesting about the clothes. I always tried to relate to them like they were my own. I tried to feel really comfortable in them. And I think through runway it started happening for me. People started seeing me and saw that I had a certain individual style. And then they began to trust me more for photography. So I began to get editorial assignments. And that happened through runway. Because in runway I was always a little sloppy and, you know, falling off the runways. It wasn't intentional. It was during a Jeffrey Banks fashion show. I always do strides as I walk. Well, I was really walking too fast. It was a tall runway and the lights were too bright. I couldn't see the end of the runway and the lights were right in my face and then I realized that I was at the end of the runway.

It's hectic behind the scene as models help
each other make rapid changes. (Left to right) Bob
Pittard, Tony Spinelli, Tony Sanchez and Denis
La Marsh. Photo: Palma Kolansky

I did a fast turn but I had on these new leather-soled shoes and one shoe went over the edge. I went backward into the audience, a six-foot drop. But I never missed a beat. I got right back up, swung myself up on the runway like I was jumping over a fence, got up, unbuttoned my coat, did a twirl and walked off. Biggest applause I've gotten."

Catalog work is the most lucrative, but it can be a literal pain. It has been described as "standing around with pins up your ass." The prototypical catalog shot is a model posed like a Bobby Doll and looking just as plastic. The clothes are pinned or padded by stylists so not one human wrinkle (or pin) is in camera sight. The shots are used in company catalogs or in newspapers to sell the merchandise. The photographic plan is, clothes in the forefront, model in the background; the merchandising plan is, sell the clothes, not the model.

"In catalog shots, you have to be a mannequin. In all respects," says Jeff Rowland. "They dress you, they pin you. They don't want any personality. They tell you what to do and what kind of look they want. Then you do your regular twelve poses or whatever. You bend your leg weirdly, you twist your body. No matter how bad it hurts, you keep that fake smile on your face."

"You concentrate on getting the wrinkles out by contorting your body but you're still supposed to look natural," elaborates Jack Mayhall, smiling even as he describes his discomfort. "Then you try to pull the shot off working with your facial expressions. When you're doing slacks, and this is no joke, you might be standing there two and a half to three hours at a time in one position, or trying to. Your legs start shaking, you start perspiring under the arms; it is pretty much physical torture sometimes, it can be, it really can. Then I start thinking about sixty dollars an hour. That's what I do," his smile becoming a laugh.

Greg Bauer, who has difficulty deciding between a Tareyton cigarette ad (*I'd rather fight than switch*) and a Canada Dry ginger ale campaign (shot in a sparkling Colorado rapids) as his favorite, has no difficulty recalling the trepidation he felt facing his first catalog assignment: "I was terrified to go to this particular studio because I had heard so many stories. Someone would mention the studio and everyone would start quaking. There was a story about a girl fainting on the set. When she woke up, she was in a different outfit. And they had her posed."

While catalog work can be dreary, many catalog models outearn the "stars" in the magazines who are obtaining editorial rates and smashing tear sheets. From an economical standpoint, catalog work is not to be scoffed at. "I am very often given the worst clothes to put on because the client feels I can sell them and make them look good," says Denis La Marsh. "I have a lot of repeat clients because in Christmas catalogs and things like that clients watch what model wears what and how much is sold. Luckily, I seem to be able to sell a lot of what I put on. So I get a lot of repeat business."

The smart model considers himself foremost a businessman. "People don't understand that being a model is being a salesman," states Ted Dawson. "My job is to sell either what I've got on my back or in my hands, or what I'm representing. If someone puts a shirt on me, photographs and publishes it, and if that shirt doesn't sell, the client won't book me again. He's going to try another salesman who sells."

With certain photographers, however, the description "catalog model" is a complete turn-off. Barry McKinley, a photographer credited with launching the careers of many leading male models, says that models who concentrate on catalog work "lose their charisma. That has a lot to do with the kind of work they do and how their agents handle them. The agents send them out every day to do boring work, then after a while they become boring. Agents don't say, 'Okay, every month you should try to do X amount of pictures to get off on for your own head, even though it isn't financially rewarding. Then devote the rest of your time to making money.' The agents are greedy. And the models get greedy. They start to work constantly and all they do is mediocre work, one after another. And they don't try to do good pictures. Models should pick and choose their jobs a little bit. But they don't, which is a pity. Then their job is just X amount of dollars at the end of the month. Some models, the first editorial job that they do is their peak. Which is sad to say."

In recent years among more advanced firms, catalog work has shed some of its "Say cheese" connotations. The photography has loosened up considerably and has taken on many of the characteristics of editorial work.

Publicity work can be a very vague area. Models may be hired by designers or manufacturers to be photographed so that press kits can be mailed to print editors in hopes that the editors will publish stories

about the sender along with the enclosed photographs. In the world of men's fashion, two major selling seasons exist—spring and fall—and clothing lines are introduced, and publicized, well in advance of the selling period. For example, spring clothes are photographed during the fall or winter months, fall clothes during the spring or summer. "The really uncomfortable time is shooting fall in summer," says Eddie Davis. "In Dallas, it is up in the nineties, a hundred or a hundred and two degrees. Getting out, shooting on location in fur coats and trying not to sweat, trying to look fresh, when you are just soaking on the inside, it is really hard." Shooting lightweight spring clothes in wintry Chicago is no joy either. Publicity photographs may appear to be very editorial or in the catalog vein, depending upon the client and photographer.

Commercial work is basically print advertising, as opposed to television commercials. The ads may be fashion ads or, more frequently, for nonclothing products. Liquor, cigarettes and male grooming aids are products that command premium rates and in many cases exclusive contracts. Fashion models are often employed in these advertisements, be they for newspapers, magazines or billboards. Other product categories—foods or tools, for example—are often cast with "funny faces" and "real people" who are listed with talent agencies, rather than with fashion models associated with fashion agencies.

Television commercials, strictly speaking, are not considered the model's province but the actor's. Most fashion agencies have separate divisions for print and television. Size requirements are less rigid in television, but the competition is just as fierce, even fiercer because someone can make a bundle from one national ad. There is also high resentment among fashion models toward other models who consider themselves primarily actors. "I don't like actors who out of necessity become models," remarks Ted Dawson with an uncustomary sneer, "the guys who say, 'I'm an actor, I'm just doing this for the money.' Sure, we're all doing it for the money. I have no greater stakes. You want to be an actor, you do Shakespeare. But don't run down what's paying the rent in the meantime and look on modeling as a tawdry thing."

Roger Sturtevant is in charge of television casting at Norman Craig and Kummel, an advertising agency that does many television commercials using male models. He believes smarter models should direct their sights at the tube for larger financial and personal rewards.

"If someone is booked for print but a television booking comes along, the agency will cancel the print booking. Television will always supersede print because the money is so terrific," Sturtevant reports. "But if a guy comes to New York and seriously wants to model, to make that his career, if he is not picked up by, in alphabetical order, Elite, Ford, Stewart, Wilhelmina or Zoli, he is not going to have a career, in my opinion. And I'm unlikely ever to meet him. It's not that I'm lazy, but there is very little chance that I will ever need someone for a commercial

Press kit publicity shot
for designer Lee Wright.
Photo: Palma Kolansky

that I cannot find in those five agencies. With other agencies, I discovered long ago that even if a picture of a nice-looking guy comes in the mail to us, he's going to be too short, outrageously unmasculine or something else.

"Casting for commercials is really typecasting. Maybe a hundred basic stereotypes are used over and over and over again, with some variations. Since commercials are twenty-eight seconds long, you immediately have to know who these people are. They immediately have to be established as newlyweds or whatever. The actors or people who don't fit into those stereotypes are not likely to get cast."

Although Oscar-winning acting talent is not required for most television commercials, some measure of talent is, if only to get an agent, Michael Slaven remarks, "Commercial agents prefer to see someone with a resumé and an acting background. They want to see more than a face and a suit size, because they know, no matter what you look like, when you go out for a TV commercial, you're going to be handed a piece of paper, and if you can't make those words a little bit interesting, then it doesn't matter at all what you look like. The most important thing is that you can read copy. All types of faces are used for television commercials, not just 'model' faces.

"The competition is really incredible," he continues. "It usually doesn't bother me if somebody else gets a job, especially if he's not my type: if he's a dark person, dark hair, very European-looking, I don't feel the least bit competitive. But on callbacks, when it may be down to you and one other person, usually what happens is you look and act and sound just like the other person. I don't know how they make the ultimate decision. I guess it's a chemical thing. It clicks. I've had people who wouldn't speak to me for a day or two when I would get the job, which is totally absurd. But that does happen. I've also had people say to me when I was on my way to an interview, 'Oh, it's already been booked,' hoping that I wouldn't go in."

"Atmosphere" is the word used to describe a type of print job that nearly every male model finds himself involved in. He is cast as the atmosphere for a female model. As atmosphere or backup, the male might only be expected to supply a shoulder for the woman to lean on.

Renée Russo, one of the top female models in the world whose leonine hair is a trademark, says, "Of the guys I've worked with, if someone is there as background, he's there for the bucks. Most guys don't mind at all. In fact, they like it. It's like they don't really have to be there to work and yet they get the bucks. So what if it's the back of your head? There's less pressure and more fun in the shooting. Really, I think there's more male/male competition than female/male competition. Now, it's easier working with a guy who knows what he's doing. Because then we can joke about how stupid it is, standing there with a number fifty-five smile planted on our faces. It can be like a rerun,

Renée Russo
Photo: Les Goldberg

Mary Macuikas
Photo: Les Goldberg

and funny. I know there are six ways I like to look in a camera and that's that. The newer guys, they're scared, so you have to relax them, but that puts a strain on you. You try to talk to them and to relax them, but you don't want them to know that you're picking up on their nervousness. Some guys don't flow as easily as others But then, that's the same with some females. Some you just click with, others you don't. It doesn't make any difference which sex you're working with; it's who you're working with."

Mary Macuikas, another great beauty, agrees. "A good model will work with you, not against you. He will just melt in with what whatever he feels is right. With someone who is unsure of himself, it's like you're standing there and you have a big hole next to you. You have to work together as a collaboration, as one unit. I've only had one really bad experience shooting with a man. We were shooting on one of the islands. It was hot and the sun was beating down and I was feeling very weak. I asked for water, but nobody seemed to hear me. I started to feel dizzy. The guy had my arm, I asked for water, and even he didn't hear me, right? We were walking back and forth along the beach and I started to mess up the pace. He said, 'C'mon, get it together.' I turned with my fist up—this guy is *huge*—and I thought, I am going to punch this guy out. He said he was going to throw me in the water, but he didn't. We just glared at each other. He had no idea how I felt, and then he says, 'Come on, get your shit together.' Oh, yeah. You enjoy working with some men—with him, I did *not*—and with others you don't. Same as with women. I like to work with people I like, and I like most of the people in this business. But I've only dated two models. Sexual preference doesn't have much effect on the working relationship. But if you have a gay guy who all of a sudden feels attracted to you and he gets all confused, then you have confusion. Or, if you have somebody who gets uptight if a woman touches him, that's hard to work with. Usually the people I work with are professional, so things go smoothly."

Because clients consider atmosphere jobs less demanding, neophytes often start out as atmosphere *if* they are lucky: a reluctance to hire beginners is deeply ingrained. Often agents will suggest novices head for Europe, where there are more men's fashion magazines and hence more work for male models.

John McNeill went to Europe in January 1978, after modeling for three months in New York City. "In August, I was working as a carpenter on Martha's Vineyard. Bruce Weber was doing a project for *GQ* and had sent out an assistant to look for men who looked like they were brothers. When Bruce called, at first I gave him a hard time. But I liked him the minute I saw that old pickup truck rolling down the road. I went to Zoli in October with Bruce's photos. I started working right away. Then a scout for an agency in Paris was looking for men to work there. I thought it would give me a chance to enhance my book and a

chance to see the world." Off he went to Paris for three months, and in April McNeill traveled to Milan. "I was working every day. I worked for *L'Uomo* and did some ads for Armani, great work like that. In mid-August, everything comes to a screeching halt in Europe, but that's the peak season in New York. I came back to cash in on all the catalog work around. Having my tear sheets from Europe helped a lot. And about that time *Dressing Right* came out." (McNeill was the cover model for that book.) "That helped a lot, too, because it was in all the bookstores, and everybody in fashion knew about it. It was funny. Remember how Matt Collins said that after *Looking Good* came out, everybody thought he was Charles Hix? Well, the same thing happened to me. People would stop me on the sidewalk and ask for my autograph and I'd just scribble Charles Hix."

But working in Europe does not automatically turn to the model's immediate advantage. Tom Cashin, returning to New York with his portfolio of European tear sheets, met a strange and strained reception. However, he didn't follow the usual route in going to Europe in the first place. Cashin went to Ireland to compete in a step-dancing competition (learned as part of his Irish heritage, although he was brought up in Brooklyn) and decided he wanted to work abroad as a model. From Ireland, he went to London, flipped through the telephone directory and came up with the name of a model agency, and went in for an appointment. "They thought it was very funny, since the agency didn't represent men," Cashin recalls wryly, speaking so softly he's barely audible. "I finally got with an agency in London, but I didn't

work at all. I was nineteen then. I didn't have any money. Somehow or other I got to Paris. I met Jerry Hall [now a top female model] the first couple of days there and we went around Paris together and we both came back to New York during the summer of 1973. There wasn't much happening here for either of us so the two of us went back to Paris together. Jerry's career really took off and I began my long three years of working in Paris. I'd come back to New York and nothing would happen, so I'd go back to Europe again to make some money modeling. Whenever I came to New York, I'd stick it out a few months, hoping work would pick up, but it never did. Which I didn't understand. But now I do. In the photographs I brought back to New York, I was in very sophisticated, older type of situations, kind of like a playboy, with the older women in elegant gowns sitting at a bar. Beautiful photographs. Great photographs. But they were just too sophisticated for my actual age. At first I couldn't understand why I wasn't assigned that type of work in New York. I was too tall and thin to be your typical junior. Well, the truth is, here they'll use a forty-year-old model for situations like those. They won't use someone who's twenty-two."

Back in New York again, chance interceded for Cashin. He was asked by director Tommy Tune, who remembered Cashin's step dancing at a party, to audition for an upcoming musical show, *The Best Little Whorehouse in Texas*. Cashin got the part and the spotlight when he broke into his Irish step dance. He also got New York modeling assignments from that exposure.

Chance can also intercede in the form of blood relatives. Enter the Bauer brothers.

Bruce and Greg are both in their thirties (Bruce is two years older than Greg), and Brad is in his mid-twenties. Some people believe a strong family resemblance is evident among the three, while others see none whatsoever. "I think I look more like my father," Bruce says, "Greg seems to be a combination of Dad and Mom, and Brad looks more like our mother. Except Brad's looks are changing a bit and he's starting to look like Dad also. I don't think the three of us really look alike. But I think Brad and Greg look more alike." (The interviewer believes Brad and Bruce look more alike. Bruce's live-in companion, Nina, thinks Bruce and Greg look more alike.) "I have my mom's legs instead of my dad's," Bruce jokes, referring to his being the shortest of the three.

The Bauers' father is a photographer—"He does primarily wedding and family portraits, baseball clubs and that type of thing," says Greg— and their mother is his assistant. "So we were all posing since we were babies," Greg remarks half seriously.

Bruce: "What got me interested in modeling was a guy I used to hang around with in college. I thought, Gee, if this guy can do it, so can I. Dad shot some pictures—standard sweater shots of me leaning against

a tree—and I took them to the Flaire Agency. They took me. It was sort of a halfhearted effort. I had planned to go to Europe for a year anyway. I did a little bit of work in Frankfurt, but I was mainly interested in traveling and hitchhiking."

Greg: "I began modeling when I was twenty and in Europe. I'd gone over to Europe with a girl friend. We went together as students. We were only going to spend a couple months traveling around. As the time passed, we lost our homesickness and thought, This isn't such a bad place, why don't we try to stay? In Paris I met a woman who owned the largest agency in Milan at that time, who told me to come to Milan, that she was sure I could work. But it took me about a month or two even to begin to get a job. It was tough, because I was a very California surfy-looking junior and there was a very limited market for my look. I was very discouraged in the beginning. Finally, after about three months—they were very long months for me—I got a big campaign for Vespa and that just started the ball rolling. I modeled in Europe for two years."

Bruce: "After two and a half years of hitching around Europe, I went to Milan to see Greg. But he was in Greece on vacation so I stayed with his girl friend. She and I went out the first night and ran into these people at a restaurant who suggested that I do some modeling. They gave me the address of an agency. It turned out to be Greg's agency."

Greg: "I heard the story how Bruce arrived in an old pair of sandals, beat-up shirt and a pair of jeans. The ladies at the agency were writing. They dropped their pens when they saw him. They sent him right away to Toscani."

Christmas greetings from the Bauer family, with youngsters Greg (left) and Bruce. Brad, shown here at bat, was born a few years later.

Bruce: "I went to see Toscani, who is one of the greatest photographers in the world, and I was working that afternoon."

Greg: "Bruce was the perfect big-brother figure. We lived at the same *pensione*. We used to call it Peyton Pensione because it had this long hallway and in each door a whole other life was going on. A belly dancer here and a violin player there, a mad actress over there, an opera singer here, and two models who were brothers. It was crazy. Bruce was very good about helping me with pictures, putting together composites. He generally oversaw everything. And I would always ask him for advice because I knew that I could trust him completely."

Bruce: "I worked for about a year in Milan, doing a lot of TV commercials as well as print, and I decided I wanted to be an actor, so I came to New York to set up shop. I wanted to be an actor but not a starving actor. I thought I'd model to support myself. The first agent I talked to said I would not make it because I wasn't six feet. I said, 'Well, I'm five/eleven, what the hell difference does an inch make?' So I had a pair of lifts made, and got to the magical height of six feet.

You know how many times in nine years in New York I have had to use those lifts? About three or four times. And I have chosen to use them because the girl was about six feet in heels.

"The first few months in New York I just hustled around with my book and my pictures. It took me about six months to get established as a working model. I had jobs, but it took about six months before I was working at least once a day. I really worked at it. The Flaire Agency was more or less an ego trip. But after working in Italy, and ever since I came to New York, it had been my philosophy to put the business into perspective. A model is a product, a commodity."

Greg: "About the time Bruce went to New York, I returned to California to finish college. I thought I was going to model part time. I went to some agencies in L.A. and they were very abrupt. I couldn't get interviews. I couldn't even leave my book. So much for modeling part time. I had less than a semester to finish to get my degree. School was really getting to me again, these spoiled little brats at U.S.C. expounding their philosophies of life when they hadn't even been out into it. They hardly had pacifiers out of their mouths. And Bruce had been writing letters from New York saying, 'If you ever feel like working, please let me know. I've shown your pictures to everybody. They love you already.' And I'd go to bed and start picturing myself in New York and wondering what it would be like. All of a sudden everything started sparkling and tingling and sizzling in my head—*Go, go, get out, get out.* One day I just packed my bags, let Bruce know I was coming and I left Los Angeles. I lived with Bruce and Nina down in the village for about three months until I found my own place. Blew up a little air mattress every night and slept like a cocker spaniel. The three of us were living in a one-room apartment, five flights above Charles Street. I loved it. Brad came to New York about two years later."

Brad: "My coming to New York was top secret. I didn't tell my folks or brothers because I figured I'd be discouraged on both ends, told I wasn't ready for it yet. I was twenty at the time. But seeing the success my brothers had had, I thought there might be a good opportunity for me. I took a flight to Newark, and took a bus into the city. I was walking down Fifth Avenue next to Central Park and I was amazed. The noise and the hustle and the bustle. That first day I walked into Ford. Both of my feet were already in the door, so to speak. Both my brothers had been with Ford for a couple years. Joey Hunter was shocked speechless. After a while, Joey said Bruce was stopping by in an hour, so why didn't I just sit tight? Sure enough, forty-five minutes later, my brother comes bopping through the door and he froze. His face turned red, scarlet, white. He swallowed, like he couldn't say anything for half a minute. Finally he managed to get out, 'What are you doing here?' "

Bruce: "I went into the Ford Agency to pick up my check and there he was. Greg, Mom, Dad, none of us wanted him to come. Because we

The Bauer brothers have seldom all three worked together. This test shot was taken soon after Brad (right) came to New York to the surprise of both Bruce (standing) and Greg. Photo: Ken Haak

felt he wasn't ready. I guess Brad finally decided that he just had to come and he knew if he asked us, we were gonna say no. So he just came. He had a pair of cowboy boots and a toothbrush in his flight bag."

Brad: "Bruce had to leave to go to another interview. But first he gave me some addresses to go to. I had a little portfolio of pictures my parents had taken and I got a rounds list from Joey. I was on my way to my first go-see when I bumped into my brother Greg."

Greg: "I was walking down the street toward the agency and all of a sudden I saw this tall blond-haired kid waving, 'Hey, Greg,' and the first thing I thought was, Oh my God, I better get my apartment back. I asked, 'What are you doing here?' He said, 'Well, I'm going on a go-see.' I said, 'Oh my God.' I ran to the agency and called the guy I'd sublet the apartment to and said my other apartment had fallen through and that I'd return his deposit but that I had to keep my apartment. He said, 'No problem. Sorry it didn't work out.' So the day he arrived, Brad had an agency, he had a job, he had an apartment, he even had his telephone."

Brad: "Greg was really freaked out because he didn't know I was coming either. We talked for a while on the street. I was still sort of shocked being in New York for the first time. There was this old drunk leaning against a post on the opposite corner. Greg said, 'Look, Brad, if that is the worst thing you ever see in New York City, you're lucky.'"

Greg: "This big-brother thing came out in me. I knew New York. Really, I felt like I should have a baseball bat at all times. I just never wanted to see him go through the bumps. But I supposed that is how Bruce felt about me."

Brad: "My brothers taught me a lot. How to pick out good photographs. What to look for as far as lighting, features and angles. What makes a photograph tick. What photographers to see. Because at that time my book was amateur."

Greg: "We all thought it would be great working together. We couldn't wait. How much more fun could you have than working with your brothers?"

Bruce: "We've done a few fashion shows together. Only a couple print jobs. There is no jealousy hang-up or anything like that. I am happy when my brothers get jobs. And we are not the same types. I am dark and Greg is more blondish. Brad is blondish and in a younger category. No real direct competition."

Greg: "We recommend each other. I will suggest Bruce or Brad for a booking if the client doesn't think that I'm right."

Brad: "Our folks are very proud of us. They like the idea of their three boys being out there in the glamor world, so to speak, and getting a piece of the pie along the way. And making good lives for ourselves. The main thing, they are very happy to see us as individuals and as brothers in the same business being happy."

CHAPTER 4
catching on

Because of the experience with that photographer—stupidly believing I could con him out of some pictures—I learned my lesson right off the bat. Modeling is a legit business, and you're a fool if you don't keep it legit. Fortunately I wised up fast.

I was not one of those people who come in and hit New York like a tornado. I was just very consistent, and very consistent on an upward gradient. I've always been successful in the sense that I've never needed to do anything else financially. But there was not a lot of satisfaction for the first couple years because I always wanted more. I was paranoid. I always wanted to get there fast.

After the trip to the Bahamas with *GQ*, which was really a joyous trip, great fun, effortless, my next booking was for Becker Studios, a catalog house. What you were at this studio was absolutely a clothes hanger. You were told where to move and, once in that position, to stand there in that exact pose. I had to stand there for an hour and a half with plastic up my pants and around the front of my shirt, with elastic around the shirt to pull it back to get rid of the wrinkles. The pants were ripped in the back to give them the proper fall. The collar was pinned. I thought, if this is modeling, I've made the wrong decision. Becker was yelling and pushing, telling all the models how terrible we were. That was his favorite pastime, screaming at models. He was absolutely the ogre of the catalog business. The Mad Hatter. He's very dead today. Not a tear fell.

I was sweating. The lights were very, very hot. I was shaking from standing still for so long. And I was being screamed at. Of course, you learn to lessen the discomfort as you learn the techniques. You learn how to bend your knees, how to relax until it's actually time to shoot while basically still standing in that same position. You learn how to ask for a fan if you're about ready to pass out.

A week or so later I had another shooting with *GQ*, but this time it was in a studio. After the Becker job, I dreaded doing another studio booking. It was difficult not having a natural environment to rely on, to act natural in. I was standing there in front of a no-seam, which is exactly that, a sheet of paper with no seam, no nothing. I was placed in front of the no-seam with my little suit on and told to relate to the camera. I didn't know what the hell to do. My hands were ten sizes larger than normal. Every gesture was exaggerated. My knees were shaking. To make matters worse, the other model on the shooting was Loíc, who had just arrived in America from France. He was the top model in France at that time— had been for seven years—and he was magnificent. He sat in the chair watching me bumble and fumble and overdo to the point of— certainly for me—embarrassment.

My turn done, I was carried off. Loíc walked on the set and gave an effortless, beautiful performance, the performance of a professional. I just sat there and watched. I should have paid money for the lesson.

GQ kindly cut out my photos from the spread. Thank God.

After about eight months, I left Stone and went to Ford. Stone was great setting me up, great getting me out and introducing me to the business. But Ford had more clout, they had more clientele, so Ford was the next logical step.

There was a stage I went through as a beginning model. I was a very competitive model inside, but on the outside I pretended not to be. I presented myself as the nice guy who just sort of lucked into things. I was keenly aware of what was going on in the business and who was doing what, but I pretended not to care.

There was another model, a very successful model, and we had both begun at about the same time. To my eyes, this model was using people, influential people in the field, to get jobs. He socialized with them, he catered to their likes. He ran with the crowd, pleasing them. I resented his open drive and ambition to get what he wanted. Initially I felt he was more successful than I because he was selling himself, so to speak. In my eyes, his were not soulful friendships, they were

Taylor used this photograph (left) for L.A. commercial work and New York modeling. Photo: Don Lewis. He was uncomfortable doing studio sessions until learning a lesson from a top French model who later photographed him. Photo: Loíc Raout

phony friendships. I thought he was very overt at being a success-climber, while I was being very covert at climbing for success. Then we found ourselves working together.

We were both booked on a shooting in the Islands. There were about ten models in total, and I had a lot of friends on that shooting. I was a real motherfucker. I punished this poor model so coldly. I was deadly. I swung the whole shooting against him, very subtly, very coldly, very calculatingly. I was indifferent or I made one or two caustic, well-placed comments. I was being very charming to everyone else. They were actually people I liked, so that wasn't hard. And this model didn't have the credentials in friendship with these people that I had. I misused friendship and ostracized him. He didn't know what hit him. And I carried around the shame of doing that for eight years. Several months ago we were booked together for a week, and I knew I wanted to clear up the wrong I had perpetrated years ago out of professional jealousy. So we talked, he was great, and we ended up laughing—mostly at me.

Models usually work together very well on the outside because the job needs to be done. If there are ill feelings, they're usually kept under control. It takes a lot to bring them out in the open. There are a few legendary stories in this business. Like two models getting into a fistfight at a catalog house because one of them was late and he was docked for the pay for the other model who was on time. Or the fistfight between a new model who had quite a bit of success and a highly established model. That fight was in a public bar. The new model kept goading the other one, claiming he'd take over his turf. Well, he lost in that fight. He also lost about a week's work because of his bruises. But the reason those stories spread so quickly is because they are so rare.

My temples turned gray when I was twenty-five. According to the agency, my face was too young to carry the gray. So I would go to the drugstore and look for a color on the package that resembled my own hair color and I would take it home, brew it and put it on. For about two or three washings, my temples would look reasonably similar to the rest of my hair. But then they would go through wonderful changes of shades, from greens to oranges to pinks. It was, in fact, shocking. And I would forget until someone would simply fall back in amazement over this person with pink temples. I covered the gray for about five years until my face finally fell into the gray.

One shooting I particularly remember took place several years ago. It was also for *GQ*. Bruce Weber was the photographer. I was very

Taylor established the rugged unshaven look after this shooting with fellow model Randall Lawrence. Photo: Bruce Weber. Courtesy of GQ.

excited because I feel he's one of the finest photographers of men
there is. We were shooting rugged outerwear on Martha's Vineyard.
Brian was art directing. Four or five days before the shooting I was
whining and complaining that I didn't want to shave. Shaving is
one of my least favorite things in the world. I complained about
it, but this time my whining fell upon someone's ears, because Brian
said, "Well, all right, don't shave. Just shut up." He called the other
model and told him not to shave either. But the other model had a
booking the day prior to the shooting, so he had to shave. I ended
up with a lot more beard, and I kind of set the unshaven, rugged
look that caught on after that shooting.

People liked it and have since asked me if I would grow my beard
for other jobs. It's one of the looks that I have. I can look rough
and very intense. I can look very happy because I have an expressive
smile. I can photograph young or as a father. I have a wide range
of looks, which can be confusing to clients. It may sound good, and
in fact, it often is, but at times it can also confuse clients.

In October 1974, when I went home to California for Christmas,
I checked in with the Nina Blanchard Agency. I started working
like crazy. Which was great, because I'd had enough of New York.
I had always preferred California as a place to live, but I didn't know
if I could work there. Well, now I could. And I thought I'd pursue

my acting. But, as it turned out, I worked so much modeling in L.A.
that I set the acting aside yet again. I wouldn't make it to acting
interviews. I chose the instant money from modeling over the maybe
money from an acting job, *if* the interview went well. If I were free,
I'd go for the acting. So I did things like *Welcome Back, Kotter,
Cannon* and *Phyllis,* but given a choice, I'd always go for the sure thing,
a booking.

California's safer than New York. New York has more of an edge
to it, more competition. Only about ten guys work constantly in
California. If you're one of those ten, you're in great shape. I was,
and I was. But seldom was the work as exciting as it was in New
York. It just wasn't on the same level. With exceptions, of course.

One of those exceptions was Albert Watson. He had a studio in
L.A. before moving to New York. Albert and I worked together
in L.A. almost every week for two years. This is a man whose work I
admire—he is brilliant, there is no other word—and for him to
admire my work back, that's exciting. He gives you the best of you
and you damn well are going to give him the best you've got for him.
It's an exciting atmosphere to work in. The smell is exciting. The
tension is high. Not of nerves, but of excitement. It spoils you. It
makes some of your other work almost unbearable.

But it was with Albert that one of my most jolting episodes took
place. I was working at the Santa Monica pier with Albert photographing for the May Company. I was in, God, a polyester leisure
suit, probably the least flamboyant clothing around. I was walking
along the pier facing Albert's camera. A carful of teenage guys drove
by and as they lurched away they yelled out the window, *"Faggot!"*
I wasn't wearing a dress, you know? I was just this man being
photographed. But that stigma is so readily attached to this business.
I got angry, in the sense that, Man, you don't know who the fuck
I am. How dare you assume, right or wrong, who I am, simply because
I'm being photographed? In that sense, I think it's unjust. But, big
deal. It's also a given.

There are a lot of men in this business who are homosexual.
There are a lot of men in this business who are straight. There are
many more straight men entering this business than there were ten
years ago. I think that it takes guts for a man to enter this field with
that stigma attached to it. Guys who decide to go for it have got
more balls than those fuckers in the car. It takes a lot of balls to be
willing to be called a fag or a fairy and still go for what you want
to do. I admire the men in this business. They have to look to their
center, they have to look to their own values, because they know

they might be degraded and treated like second-class citizens. And yet they can say, "That's all right, I'm going for what *I'm* going for, and the only person I have to settle with is me."

Often we end up with egg on our faces. So we wipe it away. For example, most male models are never told what to do on a runway. A lot of guys are like fish out of water on a runway, so they try to make up something, anything, to get them from one end to the other. What they drop out is a sense of appropriate fun. Not so much that your personality overshadows the clothes, then you're not doing your job. It's an attitude and an enjoyment. Male models can't be flamboyant on a runway, but they can't be boring either. So what do you do? You need someone who puts on a show to direct the models prior to the show. But most shows are thrown together. You're lucky if you get your sock on and your shoe tied. Then the prompter says, "Have fun." Doing what? Trying to find the runway? Yet, when it's going right, runway work can be tops. It's show biz, folks. The electricity of a live audience.

It took me a long time to acknowledge that I was, in fact, simply successful in the field I had chosen to enter. I don't think I wanted to stop chomping at the bit. I was afraid of a letdown, I guess, some loss of adrenalin that comes from driving. I think I finally acknowledged to myself that I had made it when I taped the *Merv Griffin Show*. That was in the spring of 1978.

People had been telling me that I was a successful model. My living was certainly respectable. I worked plenty. But then Merv Griffin was planning his second show around models, and I was asked to represent the field of male modeling. I had to say, Hey, listen, *listen* to what people are saying.

I realized that I had arrived as a model. And it was scary.

—*M.T.*

There is a ladder models climb in their careers. For some, the ladder is more like an express elevator. For most, each step is steep. But models starting out usually imagine themselves charmed. Their ears perk and their fantasies fly when they hear about models who escalate to the top without a hitch. Both Jack Wetzel and Michael Holder made the trip up rapidly. Their stories are the stuff that beginners' dreams are made of.

"Right from the start, Jack had a tremendous batting average," says his agent Sharon Cooper, glancing benignly toward the model who is

embarrassed to be the subject of discussion. "He would go out just making rounds and he'd get one out of every three appointments. He started working three or four times a week in the first month."

Is Wetzel a latter-day Adonis?

"I think my clients see me as a safe bet," says Wetzel with a wry smile. "Anyone can go to Marshall Field's and buy a suit they've seen me in and say, 'I can look as good as he can.'"

"I think that's true," Cooper concurs. "Jack can go from high fashion to husband-with-wife-and-child. He is very versatile. He is not as perfect-looking as some of the other male models. You can pick him apart —his nose is a little too big; this, that and the other thing—but it all works real well."

Wetzel looks more like a solid businessman than the stereotypical model—or a farmer, his occupation before being spotted on a train and mistaken for a New York City model by a public relations director. By the time the misunderstanding was cleared up, Wetzel had the executive's business card and his encouragement to do some work for the firm. "My sister and I laughed about it for the next half hour or so on the way back home," recalls Wetzel. "My town has two hundred and fifty people. I'm the tenth child of fourteen. My father said, 'Jack, why don't you try it?' He encouraged me a lot. 'Always remember, it's very crowded at the bottom but there is plenty of room at the top,' he said. It was quite a good feeling to leave a horse or a piece of machinery, get on a plane and fly here and walk in front of a camera. I had no idea of the magnitude of the business. The work is marvelous. The people you meet. I had thought I knew all the people I would want to know for the rest of my life. You know, the people you ski with, your church friends, your horse friends. But a whole new eye opened up for me."

At thirty, Michael Holder had been employed at a San Francisco shipyard for three years while taking occasional art classes. He was working out in a local gym during March 1978 when someone suggested he stop by Model Management. "I was working three days later," Holder recounts. He went to the agency, was immediately sent to a photographer, tested that same afternoon, went to Macy's on a go-see also that same day, and was booked for his first shooting for the day following the next. "My first shot was selling a shower curtain with a towel around me," he says. "At the next shooting—a fashion shot—the stylist made me up. I looked like Donna Reed. Or Greek tragedy. I was having fun. I wanted to see how the picture turned out." It turned out well enough for Holder to get a spate of jobs. By June, he was in New York City to attend the Art Students' League. He had been told to check out Zoli Men, which he did. "Zoli had me out seeing more people in one day than there are to see in San Francisco." After living in New York for ten days, Holder joined the herd at a cattle call casting for a *GQ* cover to be photographed by Barry McKinley. Four days later

(Top) Jack Wetzel. Photo: Jerry Brody
(Bottom) Michael Holder. Photo: Herb Ritts

he was shooting the cover. "From June through August, I earned enough to meet expenses." In August, Holder worked for the Bloomingdale's Christmas catalog (art directed by Brian Burdine) and also got a ten-day booking in San Francisco shooting the Macy's Christmas catalog. "I've been making my quota every week since then. Somewhere around seven hundred to eight hundred dollars every week," Holder estimates. "Money flows through me like orange juice."

Both Wetzel and Holder's scenarios are what whets most beginning models' imaginations. So does the first part of Conrad Bell's experience, but not the second.

First Installment from Bell: "I'm from Georgia, went to the University of Georgia and got my degree in advertising design and art education. Then I packed my old Volkswagen and landed in California in 1968. I got a job immediately as a set designer, worked in wardrobe at NBC, did another stint as a set designer, got a part in a film, got an agent. There was one week when I got the lead in a TV pilot and three

commercials. Then there was a hiatus. I got tired of unemployment. Somebody said I should go see Nina Blanchard. I went there and the next week Harry Coulianos came out to cast a California issue of *GQ*. I had only been modeling for one week at that point. Mike Edwards and I got the issue. All of a sudden I had twelve pages in *GQ*. I looked like I was a model, when in actuality it was a fluke. So I came to New York a month later. I had my book with a few ads from California, plus twelve pages of *GQ*. It looked like I was a professional. My first day in town I got to do a package for a hair dryer. It was eight hundred dollars the first day and I felt this was a piece of cake."

Bell's Second Installment: "I didn't have another day booking for two years. I had hour bookings here and there, but it was two years before I got a day booking. I was doing rounds of eight to ten people a day, keeping notes on what their reactions were. Their reactions were to get you in and out. They would look through my book while they were eating tuna fish. Very discouraging. The only thing I found I could depend upon was rejection." Bell punctuates his pronouncement with an aggressive nod, his blond hair bouncing in emphasis.

Having gone through the rigors of putting together their portfolios and composites, most models are so obsessed with forging their careers that they cannot comprehend why many clients remain reluctant to book them. They may begin to doubt their own physical attributes when in fact clients are reticent for reasons related to economics.

"You save money using experienced models," believes Arnie Linsman, a public relations man who handled Pierre Cardin's men's wear for many years. "I talk from a publicity standpoint where every dollar has to count. Usually I can't afford to take chances on first-go-round models unless I'm doing a single shot, which is very unusual," he says with soft apology in his voice. "When we book models, generally we're shooting a lot of pictures and we need speed, the speed that a pro has in understanding the clothes he's wearing. The clothes may be the most beautiful in the world, but somebody standing there like a lump doesn't do much for them."

Patsy Beattie is the director of photography for catalog production house Bowman & Associates in Los Angeles. She emphasizes, with a melodic Irish accent, that knowing the techniques of catalog work is crucial. "The difference in the greater degree of professionalism between the top and lower brackets in men is greater than it is with girls, because there are fewer men at the top. The guys who have reached the top— I would say there are probably only five that I would constantly, constantly recall. I had a disco shirt to shoot the other day, and I happened to interview this model. I go out and here is this handsome blond— weak-looking, but handsome—and he has a carnation for me and a carnation for the receptionist and he is very sweet. And I am looking for someone to wear this disco shirt. I read this guy's resumé and he is

Conrad Bell
Photo: Michael O'Brien

a disco dancer on television. So I can maybe get away with a weak guy if he moves well. I book him. The bloody fellow wouldn't stop dancing. He danced his little heart out, but he wouldn't slow down and give the photographer a chance to catch him. So I got all these wrinkled shirts."

Many clients, not necessarily justly, lump all rookie models into one category. Having over the years seen new models who are inadequate for any of several reasons—the wrong look, the wrong size, the wrong attitude—certain clients develop a suspicious nature.

"Of the men we see, probably only ten percent ought to be sent here in the first place," estimates Bob Connors, head of public relations for Hart Schaffner & Marx, the men's clothing giant. "They don't have the look or they don't have the shape, they don't have the build, whatever. So many models don't even know what a size is. I will have a model come in and he'll say, 'Well, I'm a forty regular or long.' I explain that you can't be both because it isn't the cut of the garment, it's the length of your body that determines whether you're a regular or a long. You can't get that through their heads."

Connors' frown becomes a sardonic grin. "I guess some models feel that I'm the most demanding person they've ever worked for. We have gotten to the point where we now issue every new model a list of instructions about what we expect. One of the rules is if we're doing a three-model shot and a model is half an hour late with no good reason, then that model pays the other models for their half hour. Some people say, 'Well, that's unheard of.' I say, 'Sorry if it's unheard of, that's the way we operate.' We even get down to the type of underwear the model should wear. (The bikini type, very tight and constricting.) As I say in the instructions, 'You can let it all hang out on your time, but not on ours.'

"Once a new model came to my office. I have them change right in my office; we do not stand on ceremony. I always give them the option of going into the men's room if they're the bashful type. Well, the model kept looking over the partition to see if anyone was watching him. I had him try on the trousers, too, because that's a vital part of the suit. No underwear. Well, I was dumbstruck. This had never happened to me before. I didn't say anything, I didn't know *what* to say. Now, forewarned, forearmed. Anyone who has the audacity to put on somebody else's clothes without underwear gets told to go home and get his underwear and come back. Usually they don't because they're embarrassed."

Still shaking his head in disbelief, Connors continues. "Some guys have so much attitude. I remember in particular one new model we'd never used before. He came in and I said, 'We'd like a fitting but I do want to mention your hair is too long for this shot. Would you have it trimmed?' And he said, 'No, this is my hair, you take it as it is.' I answered, 'I don't have to take it as it is. You take your hair and leave.'

It isn't as if his hair wouldn't grow back. If he'd said, 'I prefer my hair this length and I really don't want to cut it, so maybe you don't want to use me,' that would have been fine. But, 'This is my hair, you take it or you lump it.' We lumped it."

Jobs may also be sluggish in coming because of the new model's inexperience with interviewing.

Vicky Pribble, a booker at the Zoli agency, states, "When men start modeling, some of them take only a month to get it together; others, six months or a year. I've had some fabulous guys who took a year, two years to get to the point where they were really earning money. And some guys not so good, maybe, can go out and make a lot of money right away because, one, they really want to make a lot of money, and two, they are easy about walking into studios and meeting clients, it doesn't throw them at all. They are easy, present themselves well, and they work."

Paul Rogers, who books great numbers of models in his capacity as men's fashion director for Sears, says, "Beginning models in particular don't know the basics of handling the business. Time after time a new model will show up at the desk and expect to be seen. All models should call ahead, as in any other business. And, of course, then be on time. As far as the fashion model is concerned, if that's the image he's trying to project, then he should approach some type of fashion look when he comes in. That doesn't mean he has to go out and buy a new suit or even be in a suit. But he certainly shouldn't come in wearing a T-shirt and jeans and try to sell you on the fact that he's a fashion model. Especially in the beginning, because most beginners don't have a multitude of shots to show you how they look in different outfits. Much of the time you have to take beginners at face value."

"I think it pays to have something interesting in the portfolio, something funny or strange, maybe, but something interesting to talk about," notes Ken Baker, a master of nonchalance. "A lot of photographers are very insecure, they may not even want to see male models. They will sometimes send for your book rather than see you personally. I've seen a lot of insecure art directors too, who are nervous because they've

Ken Baker
Photo: Bill Farrell

heard stories that all male models are homosexual or what have you. Having something interesting in the book can set off a conversation and break the ice."

When interviews are not generating bookings, the difficulty may be a weak portfolio. That means back to the testing trail, where photographers may still be elusive.

"A model really has to have some charisma, sexual or whatever," analyzes Barry McKinley, fingering his red mustache. "You can cut his hair or change his clothing, but if the charisma isn't there, you can't give him that magic. All of the great models I've worked with are usually the plainest people. They have much more fantasy about themselves and a sense of humor about themselves. They are not the ones who take your breath away when you see them. In fact, very few of those people make it. The magic is there or it isn't. I want magic in every shot."

New York photographer Les Goldberg, describing what he wants in a model, says, "Essentially what I'm looking for is the elements of personal style. Just putting on a garment is not the ability to project an image. The model must have something to contribute to the garment, to the look, to be able to create an ambiance. I find the male models whom I like to work with are those I can project my own fantasies onto and get a shot back the way I would love to see myself in that situation. Something behind the face. What makes an extraordinary model is that model's passion for what he's doing. If you do it for the money or you do it to get somewhere else, you're not doing it because you want to be wonderful at modeling."

Though the model has been indoctrinated in testing, even time's passage doesn't make testing child's play. Frustrating incidents, like

Murphy's Law, have ways of recurring. For example, nude shooting proposals don't diminish. Rick Williams, a former construction crew foreman with some ingrained fears more than offset by a great desire to shift career gears and make a go of modeling, had been testing off and on for several months when "I ran into a photographer who said, 'Oh, yes, I'd like to do some testing with you. Would you like to do some nudes? And if we test, we have to do some nudes.' So I went home and waited it out and said, 'Shit, I'm never going to know unless I go ahead and do it.' So I went ahead and did it and I got the contact sheet back. The majority of the frames were out of focus." His laugh sounds like a German shepherd's bark. "But doing nudes didn't affect me one way or the other. I just did it."

Not that there is necessarily anything licentious about nude work. For a large number of models, the sensuality of the experience is totally pleasurable. Some find that working nude helps them to work in clothes. "I used to do nude tests," relates Kalani Durdan. "I was very uptight when I started in front of a camera. All of a sudden I had hands hanging beside me and I didn't know what to do with them. I never noticed my hands until I got in front of a camera. A photographer told me that when I could deal comfortably in front of a camera nude, I would be totally relaxed with clothes on. We spent a couple hours in his studio. I just walked around totally nude, talked on the telephone, read, made cold drinks and he just took pictures of me. That did help me in front of a camera more than anything else."

Nude shots can also have some unexpectedly funny consequences. Joe MacDonald did a nude shooting with Skrebneski in 1976. What prompted him to do the shooting? His mother. "My mother said, 'I

(Opposite) production number with (left to right) Michael Taylor, Randall Lawrence, Ted Dawson and Bob Clement. Photo: Les Goldberg. (Above left) Kalani Durdan. Photo: Bruce Weber. (Right) Rick Williams. Photo: Michael O'Brien

think you should do it. You'll want it someday,' " MacDonald says. "He did one roll and the picture was, I thought, incredible. I loved it. It was used in an exhibition of Victor's photography at the Chicago Art Institute. I didn't see it, but it was blown up ten feet high. My mom is very witty. Victor told me that when she went to the show and saw that photograph, she said to Victor, 'I didn't realize Joe had such big'—long pause—'muscles.' "

A beginning model's attitude toward the profession and his commitment are constantly second-guessed by clients, particularly those who book models regularly. They resent models whose sole aspiration is to pluck golden apples without bothering to climb the tree. As Harry Costas Coulianos remarks, "When I find new people coming up, fresh new faces, naturally I look at their books to see how they photograph and imagine how they would look in certain situations. But I like to talk to them. I like to see their views of themselves, whether they have assurance about themselves, and, most important, why they are doing what they are doing. Do they really want to model or do they want to get off on it for their egos? I feel a responsibility to the people who really want to be male models and who want to make a livelihood and give of themselves. It's a very hard job. A very difficult thing. It takes a lot of self-sacrifice, there's an awful lot of shit. I don't want to invest the time, to give the opportunity to somebody who's going to throw it away."

When models don't feel their careers are catching on fast enough, to inflate their flagging confidence they often look for a target—possibly a scapegoat—to wreak their aggressions on. Their agencies are convenient sitting ducks. The constant complaint is that every agency has its favorites, a select crew that is sent from go-see to go-see and that lands the lion's share of jobs.

Jimmy Grimmé admits, "No matter what agency a model belongs to, an agent gets in the habit of automatically picking models who are always, constantly used. They are not necessarily his pets. He may not even like them personally. But they are the ones who come to mind because they are the most visible. You get a new model who is really sensational, of course you will start pushing immediately for that new model. You hope every model you take on is going to the top, otherwise you wouldn't take someone on, but, let's face it, it's show biz. I like to have my models come into the agency. That way, the newer ones with a good but not that exquisite a look, I'm reminded of them. All of a sudden the phone starts ringing and a client leaves the model selection to me. Joe Doe's sitting there. Snap, Joe, go on over. But, truthfully, the tendency is to go with the established model, because you feel your chances are better of pleasing the client."

Seldom does the agent have more than a weak voice in deciding who gets a booking. The final say is always the client's. Repeat business contributes a hefty portion to a successful model's income. "The established models who are already working have set clients, people who call in to book them two or three months ahead," remarks Vicky Pribble, her voice cheery. "It can be very crazy at the agency. You want to sell everybody, but there's nothing in the world like sitting at a telephone with five lines on it when all five are ringing, which is always. On all five lines are clients wanting different models at different times, and most of them are crazy and screaming that they have budgets. They ask for so-and-so and so-and-so is booked. Here's a good opportunity to say I have somebody who's new and terrific. But usually photographers play it safe because they have their budgets and their clients who are particular and conservative and scared. Many photographers would like to think they've made a great find, but they can be intimidated by the client. I can talk up the new guys, but not everyone will listen."

Even models working regularly can fall into the trap of comparing their bookings to other models'. Randall Lawrence, whose thick thighs and calves ("I have felt like a freak, a distorted freak at times," he says with a hearty guffaw) have not interfered with his lucrative career, points out, "Even today, if I go into the agency and start looking at other charts, I'll just start to freak myself out. I always imagine other guys are working more than I am, even if they're not." Yet models with only several months experience find the temptation to compare their work loads irresistible. The larger agencies represent upward of seventy men. Newer models fear their identities will get lost in the shuffle of headsheets.

The model-agent relationship can be a touchy affair. The traditional line is that the model is the client and the agency works for him, not vice versa, because without models an agency could not survive. Not a bad *theory*, but without agents, most models wouldn't work. When registered models are persistently without work, the symbiosis is endangered. "Since agencies are going to take money anyway, I would give them thirty percent if they would make more money for me," claims Charles Williamson, his normally placid, Jamaica-tinged voice harsh. "I *should* pay them, just as long as they work for me. I work very hard. I didn't get where I am by sitting around and letting an agent do for me. If I had, I wouldn't be in this business at all now. It tends to piss me off when agents take a percentage and don't do anything. If I am working, they should make sure that I keep working. For their prestige, they should make sure their models work."

Once a model is on firm ground, it generally matters little with which agency he is registered. Clients have favorite models and will book them whatever their affiliation. But until a model's career has caught on, the crux is whether any agency does enough to launch him. Most models who have scaled the top, credit their rise to their own persistence or their own good fortune. They may have close and cordial relationships with their bookers, but deep down, despite the hugs and pecks on the cheeks, many models feel they've done it pretty much on their own.

The agency may have supplied a helpful push, but the real sweat has been the model's, is a widespread assessment.

"The agencies take on too many kids and promise them the moon," observes Barry McKinley. "Actually, I don't know any agency in New York that really knows how to get new people together and get them motivated. It is more the photographers who supply the agencies with the talent rather than the other way around."

"When a male model has been with a top agency for a period of three months, even though the agency is known to do a lot for its models, I think the good male model will undertake his own PR at that time," suggests Ken Baker, who runs an acting/modeling school—The Classic School—in Manhattan. "I frankly don't think that the top agencies have the time to do a lot for a model after three months. Modeling is big business. It's up to a model to take notes in his diary and rely on himself to follow up when he meets a photographer or art director on go-sees. Relying solely on one's agency is a mistake. Frankly, agencies don't have the time to work with the individual."

Agencies retort that they do indeed play their part, a vital one, in setting up appointments, sending out composites and headsheets, and by talking up their men. Their efforts drum up *potential* business, they insist, but if the model lacks motivation and drive, he'll ultimately screw up. Persistence may not always pay off, but there's no payoff without persistence. Every agent has scores of stories about models who were treated like leprosy patients for months by clients but who suddenly for no apparent reason caught on. Motivation? Luck? Destiny? Perseverance? An agent's efforts hitting pay dirt? Who knows? The unpredictability of the business is ruthlessly predictable. Michael Edwards, whose resemblance to James Dean was once considered a liability, became an instantaneous hot property after he was photographed for a Johnson's Baby Oil campaign—but he had spent a year and a half preparing for that instant.

"I spent a year in New York and did only about six jobs during the whole year," Edwards recalls. "Nina Blanchard asked if I'd be interested in coming to California and I said sure. I came out here and starved also. But a few months after I got here, Richard Noble came out to shoot a spread for Johnson's Baby Oil. That was before Ali McGraw was an actress. Noble shot Ali McGraw, myself and two other guys. It was a big two-page spread in *Seventeen*. It was very beautiful, and when that came out, Michael Edwards was on the map. I looked at that ad and gulped, wondering if it was me. The phone rang and Nina said, 'Get your ass over to this office. Get a shave. The phones haven't stopped ringing for you.' They never stopped."

"Every model has to pay what we all call his dues," remarks Denis La Marsh. "I would say it's usually a year before you start to see any results. For me, let's say it took, from when I started, almost a year

before I really started seeing any money, when I could support myself—meagerly, but I could still support myself."

After his dues have been collected, the model can give up his part-time job waiting tables, driving taxis on the night shift or whatever else he's been doing to keep body and board together. Now he really starts to learn his craft; the only way modeling skills are acquired is through regular work.

On-the-job training can be fun. "There were three of us in the shot," relates Mark Shapiro. "We were going to shoot in Central Park, but it

(*Above*)
"*The Beard,*"
Denis La Marsh
Photo:
Les Underhill
(*Right*)
Mark Shapiro
Photo:
Tom Clayton

was raining and the client needed the shots right away, so we worked in the studio. Studio shots can be dull and uninspired because, after all, you're just standing there and there's nothing much to relate to. I was standing at one end. Just as the photographer started to shoot, the guy on the other end just slammed into the guy in the middle, who unexpectedly almost knocked me three feet in the air. I realized, hey, that was really a good thing to do, actually. I really got into it. I started pushing back the other way. It was very spontaneous. The guy in the middle thought it was a football game. I'm glad I wasn't in the middle. The shot had life in it. Otherwise it would have been a picture of three deadbeats. Smiling."

Models experiment with different techniques to psych themselves up for the camera. One model has his own method of achieving a stern, penetrating look: "I hum 'St. Louis Woman' and fantasize the biggest cock I can imagine."

Others go through more metaphysical exercises. Larry Harmon, one of Dallas's most successful models, says, "For me personally, I look at that camera and say, 'That camera is the world. It represents all the people who are going to see this picture.' In order to communicate with those people out there, I have to look through that lens onto the film and think about what this shot is going to look like once it comes out in print. If you don't project yourself through that lens, then somewhere between you and the flash, you're going to lose it. Models who are successful at this business often change completely when the camera starts rolling. They move differently than when they're walking down the street. You go somewhere else in your head, and you project a different image of yourself. Otherwise, people might as well watch people walk down the street and have a fashion show and try to pick the models."

With techniques and confidence both on the upswing, shootings can become more pleasurable. Albert Watson recalls an extremely memorable shooting. He walks and jumps as he re-creates the scene, acting each role himself. His Scottish burr becomes more pronounced as the

Larry Harmon
Photo: Constance Ashley

story unfolds. "The plan was for these three men to stand in a row, looking very cool, very macho, wearing the latest miniature bikini briefs. I said to the guys, 'Okay, get ready.' At that time we had a couple of girl assistants in the studio. The briefs were *brief* and I didn't want the men to be embarrassed. So I said, 'Okay girls, out.' This was a few years ago, nowadays I can't believe I did that. I went out to pick up some coffee and yelled in, 'Are you ready?' And the guys said that they were, so I came back in with my coffee, and they were all sitting down, talking with each other, in bikini briefs. And I repeated, 'Ready?' 'Yup.' So I got behind the camera, and all three men got up and stood there with their arms folded. I looked through the frame, checked it, checked their faces, began shooting. I did a couple frames and to my horror noticed the crotch of the man in the middle. Well, I've seen a few crotches in my life, but this was obscene. I bolted up with horror. I thought. My God, what am I going to do? Then suddenly they all laughed. Of course, when I'd gone out to get my coffee, they'd stuffed socks down the front of the underwear. The real laugh in this must have been my face, that look of absolute horror. Sure, we were all friends, but I'd never seen them in bikini briefs. And there was the guy in the middle, just more endowed than God ever meant mortal man to be." His *tour de force* completed, Watson plops down on the sofa, chuckling, receiving one solid clap of applause from his wife, Liz.

Sometimes the joy comes from nonprofessional onlookers. Ken Baker tells of a shooting that simulated newlyweds emerging through the church doors. He too becomes increasingly animated, using body language to color his tale. "We had a limousine, we had a chauffeur, we had the little boy and the little girls all dressed up as part of the wedding. The best man and all that. The photographer was about a hundred yards away using a telephoto lens, so I couldn't hear the clicks. We came down the steps, we couldn't hear the clicks but we knew he was shooting and we just continued the action. We stopped at the bottom of the steps and kissed this long kiss. There were a couple of mock photographers taking pictures, but there was no film in their cameras. And then we went to the car. I put the bride in the car and I walked around to my side of the car and got in. As we started to pull away, a little old lady came up and she was crying, she was really broken down. She was crying so much that I rolled down the window. She said, 'You look so beautiful together I hope you spend the rest of your life this happy.' Then we drove around the block. When we came back to the church, she was still there, still crying. Her whole world was shocked when she realized as we went back and repeated the action that it was all for photography. Ten minutes earlier she was crying over this beautiful scene, ten minutes later she was in shock."

While some jobs are lighthearted, others are decidedly heavy, often because of the atmosphere on the set. "I had a situation with a photographer who I felt was very pushy, very insensitive," says Mark Shapiro.

"I think if it happened again, I'd probably deck him. I was very new at the time, and I wasn't feeling all that confident about this new business. It was a double shot, and the girl was feeling it as well. It was a power trip on the photographer's part. He wasn't as abusive toward her as he was toward me. It was tone and innuendo. More than, 'Mark, you stupid ass.' More taunting, like, 'What's the matter, Mark, don't you know how to hold a woman?' The thing was, I was very new and I felt that I needed that shot. It was a full-page color shot, and I needed that for my book. Today, I'd deck him."

That models may be moved like inanimate props takes its toll. "I really used to enjoy modeling," recalls Scott MacKenzie. "Then all of a sudden it struck me one day, I am not the artistic one in the shooting. Just because I am on the film, I am not controlling the art aspects of it. When that happened, it kind of burst my bubble."

Some of the novelty of the work drops off. Even though a model's earnings may be steadily increasing, so too can his frustration at having always to remain even-tempered in the face of real or imagined disparagement.

"There are always games," believes the usually amiable David White. "The way clients treat you. The power games. I can't tell a client, 'Go fuck yourself,' because maybe I will never work for him again. I think a model should be able to say, 'You can't do this to me.' If the client is going to blow up at me, I should be able to turn around and tell him, 'I am not a piece of meat. You might have me for the day, but I am not your piece of meat to treat anyway you want to.' In almost any shooting, the model is treated the worst."

Sometimes the drive to retaliate cannot be detoured.

Scott MacKenzie admits to being "temperamental," despite the business axiom: Modeling has no room for temperament—you can always be replaced. MacKenzie mentions a particular episode, relishing the telling if not the living:

"Last summer it was ninety-seven degrees out and I was doing Shetland coats with turtleneck sweaters, one hundred percent wool. I was dressed as if it were a hundred below, not a hundred above. The humidity was incredible and I was standing in the middle of a field, dripping wet. I took it all day until the last shot when the art director said, 'I want my dog in the picture.' And he wanted to direct the dog. 'Do this, Lady, do that.' I just went crazy. I kicked the dog, pushed the art director down, threw off the sweater and coat and ran and sat in the car. Locked myself in. I just went freaks. But I have seen the guy since and now it is a laughing matter."

One more explosive incident. Conrad Bell, more volatile at times, more ingenuous at others than the typical model, was doing a runway show. "I was busting my ass over hairdressers and everything to get back to change my clothes—there were no dressers—and to get back on stage. I've always resented people with power who come off loud and

Clayton Landey
Photo: Guy Luzoro

pushy but aren't professional, which personifies the woman I was doing the show for. So, there I am busting my ass and I'm waiting in the wings to go on. I'm *waiting*, but no one cues me. Finally I hear, 'Conrad, Conrad, I am here,' and with that she pushes me toward the stage like a piece of meat and says, 'You are late.' Now I have been waiting for almost five minutes through all this confusion backstage. So I just took the clothes off in front of her and said, 'You show the clothes.' "

Resentments about money also pop up. The tales of pots of gold can seem a crock. Models report that certain clients can't tell time.

"I was doing a shoot with this particular photographer," recollects Atlanta model Clayton Landey, fidgeting in his chair. "I arrived on time, but he didn't have his lights ready for two hours. Then the stylist wasn't so crazy about the woman's hair. So the hairdresser fooled with her hair for another hour. My agency had told me I was on an hourly rate, but then the client said, no, I was on a half-day rate. Terrific. By now we're already three hours into my four-hour half-day rate. By the time the shooting's over, it took five hours. And the photographer said, 'Oh, I was only budgeted for a half-day. Sorry, I can't pay you any more.' I said, 'Wait a minute.' I tried to talk to him and he said, 'Fine, talk to the art director.' She was a real strong woman, wow. I said, 'If I'm not worth my published rate, why did you hire me?' And she said, "Well, Clayton, if you're going to push me on every little thing, I know the next time around I'm not going to hire you.' I didn't get paid the extra and I haven't heard from her since. Maybe it's a bad habit, but I'm not an ass-kisser."

As do most models, David White has a similar story, but one with a real kicker. "If I work for seven hundred and fifty dollars a day, I'm not the kind of model who will charge an extra hour overtime unless a client is giving me a real hard time and I know he deserves the charge. This was in California. I did an ad and I charged an extra thirty-seven fifty. The client got furious. I mean furious. The money was mine. I earned it. And I found out after the ad appeared that weekend that the store made forty-two thousand on this one product in all the stores."

"If I could change one thing about the modeling business," muses Loíc Raout, his cat eyes studying the ceiling, "I wouldn't pay the models by the hour. I would give a percent per page. One day I was working for this big company and I liked the shirt. I said to the client, 'Can I buy this shirt?' The client said, 'Oh, you models are all alike, you make so much money and you always want something for nothing.' I said, 'Don't pay me. Just give me point one percent of the money you're going to make out of the ad you're shooting right now, instead of paying me for three hours,' and he answered, 'Yeah, you're right; I would give you sixty-five thousand dollars.' The model's job is to make magic and money out of whatever the client puts on his shoulders. The client spends a couple hundred dollars for the model's fee and stands to make hundreds of thousands of dollars out of the shooting."

And while the model's hourly rate looms large beside that of many a blue-collar or even white-collar worker, only the super-charged dynamos work daily. "And what about the fifteen or twenty or thirty minutes in travel time to get to and from a job?" asks Ed Fry, a top earner in Dallas who also works in San Francisco. "Then there's the hour or two it took to prep for the job. Maybe the hour that you had to spend finding the particular piece of clothing you were asked to bring. Maybe it is the money you spend to get particular clothing cleaned so that it looks crisp and photogenic. I am a businessman. I have overhead just like every other businessman. I have to pay my agent. I pay the government taxes every three months. Nobody is paying my medical insurance. I don't get benefits, such as free dental care or breaks in auto insurance. I don't get any of that, it all comes out of my own pocket. So my expenses as a businessman are just as much or more than anybody else's. McGraw-Hill would tell you if you were a salesman that you need to value your time at seventy-two fifty an hour in order to at least break even, and that includes transportation time, any type of overhead expense. They were talking about salesmen. Well, I'm paid sixty dollars an hour. If their facts and figures are true, you tell me where that puts me?"

The promise of big and fast money is often an empty one. And the emptiness that follows rejection is always imminent. "If you let your personal ego and your professional ego come together, you go crazy," suggests Brian Collins, one of San Francisco's successes. "Even if you're

making a bundle, you get rejected so often that you're gonna feel like you got coal in your Christmas stocking. But if you go into an interview and give it your best, leave and forget about it, then you'll be well. Then, if you get a call, it's a wow. I don't go in thinking I'm going to get the job or I'm not going to get it. I go in feeling prepared and knowing that I'll give it my best shot. There are so many reasons for not being chosen. Maybe you look like the client's brother-in-law and he hates him. Maybe he doesn't like what you're wearing, your clothes are too straight. There are so many reasons for not being chosen. Conversely, there are so many reasons for being chosen as frivolous as the ones for not being chosen. It's capricious."

The capriciousness can border on the absurd. What's in a name? In the case of lanky Tony Sanchez, a certain client's inability to see him

(Opposite) Brian Collins. Photo: Paul Gremmler
(Above) Tony Sanchez. Photo: Bruce Weber

clearly. "I am Hispanic in background but not in image. In fashion work, my name has only once been a problem. There was a midwestern client who refused to see me any other way than Hispanic. This was after meeting me, talking with me and spending time with me. He insisted I was Hispanic. Period. Both of my parents are Spanish, but I don't convey that image of what people think of as either Puerto Rican or Mexican-American. In the commercial field, it is more difficult because people wanted to slot me with my name. I refuse to go on some commercial agents' calls anymore because I would walk into a casting session and everybody was speaking Spanish. I don't even speak Spanish."

The capricious aspects of the profession are rivaled by its competitiveness. The honed edge of competition can whittle away at ingrained personality patterns.

"This business, especially in New York, is dog-eat-dog," David White says. "You know, a dig here and a few digs there. You just have to watch out what you do and what you say. A lot of people just want to use you, and when they are through with you, they will just kick you out. I have grown up. Being here has taught me a helluva lot that I never would have learned in Tennessee or Florida. I was always open. Always willing to help and always willing to talk. Now, I just stay back and remain very quiet. I am very careful."

Close contact with schemers can make one wary. One model freely says, "I'll suck doorknobs to make it." A thought—and an image—repulsive to most serious models. Although friendships with fellows are formed, the depth of the affection may be suspect. When guards are lowered, sometimes the unthinkable occurs. "I had a very good friend," remembers Chicago-based Jon Gilmore. "He is a pretty big model with the leathered face, the whole thing. We were kind of up for the same job. A shirt manufacturer was doing some tests for a good contract. My hair was kind of long, so he gave me a haircut so I could make this go-see. Fool that I was, I trusted him. After he cut my hair, I looked like something out of a concentration camp. I felt like the village idiot for letting that happen. And he admitted that he did it on purpose."

Although models claim a great *esprit de corps*, bitchiness and back-biting are not outside the ranks. "I would say there is more jealousy with the guys than there is with the girls," assesses Nina Blanchard. "Little digs, you know. For example, there was a new guy doing a Calvin Klein show. I watched the way the guys backstage reacted to him. We had some big guys in that show. Mike Edwards was darling with him, he couldn't have been more helpful. But there was another guy, who will be nameless, the prick, and, boy, was he frosted. 'How did he get here?' the shmuck asked within the new guy's hearing. He treated him like dirt, wouldn't talk to him. Everybody noticed it."

Difficulties coping with the profession can cause hardships handling one's personal life. Todd Starks, a San Francisco model, blames the dissolution of a marriage, if not wholly at least partially, on the strain of spending as much or more energy on his modeling career as on matrimony. Like many models who prefer emphasizing only the profession's positive angles, Starks is visibly disturbed exposing the sore points. Yet, after airing the wounds, he exhibits the resilience characteristic of most models. The smile returns, the shoulders are squared, the handshake is resolute. The public persona is intact. But, for a while, private feelings are reflected in a quiver of the voice or a cast of the eye.

"A couple years ago I met this girl, a stewardess, in Los Angeles," Starks begins. "I had been planning to run a little streak up here and then to move into the L.A. market. I'd been in the business about eight months. Looking back, I know I wasn't professionally ready for Los Angeles. But there was this girl and I'd had a bit of success up here and figured, okay, I'm going. So off I went to L.A. and moved in with her. Well, you couldn't say I was successful right off the bat. I was getting pressure from her to cool the career, to move into a straight life, a straight job. The pressure from not working well in L.A., plus from her, was getting me down real bad. We went on like this for about six months. But she was real great. I did have a straight job up here, which was really a good deal, I could come and go as I pleased. And in L.A., I didn't work enough to cover my expenses at all. So I decided to come back to San Francisco. She came with me. We got married.

"But still the pressure was there to stop modeling and acting, to stick with a straight job. Initially I almost had to do that because I'd run out of money in Los Angeles and I had to get refinanced again. So I was taking modeling jobs only here and there when the agency called, but I was not out hustling or seeing photographers. I was working maybe

Todd Starks
Photo: Charles Jackson

once a month. Of course, most of the time when I was working or test-ing, I was doing it with women. She got all worried that I might be straying, running around with these other women. I got my finances straightened out, well enough to believe that I could take more time off from my job and start actively pursuing modeling and acting. I wasn't going to take the baloney of her pressuring me to get out of the business. So I sat her down and told her, 'Listen, I'm going to start working again. I'm going to work at it, I'm going to push, and I'm going to make it.' On the surface, she claimed she was accepting of the whole thing, was behind me one hundred percent.

"But getting back into it after inactivity for a year, well, I had to start over again. I had to test again and again, because my look had changed to a degree. And I started testing with women and alone also. She was upset that money wasn't coming in from my job and that I was testing with women. And I had started taking acting workshops. This fueled it more because I was rehearsing with women at night. There was a lot of tension in the situation. It could never be alleviated. Even though I started working as a model.

"Several months ago it all broke loose. I couldn't handle the pressure of her thinking I was screwing around with all these other women. So we got a divorce.

"I don't know what she's doing now.

"Especially when you're starting out, the career has to come first.

"I'd say that the majority of models in the business, if they're hooked up with someone outside the business, and if that person isn't completely loose and doesn't give a complete free rein, then there's going to be a hassle. I can think of only one guy in this agency who's married and very happily married, and his wife doesn't hassle him at all. But, gee, I'm not sure I know of any other model who's married. Modeling is not real conducive to being married."

While the model's mode of living may be in flux (his emotions, too), he is likely to feel the brunt of others' hostility. Bruce Bauer admits, "On occasion I have felt the need to defend myself, say at a party. I remember a girl coming up to me. It is either jealousy or maliciousness. She knew that I did modeling, and she came up to me and said, 'Oh, you are one of those people who make their living off their looks.' I just said, "Well, honey, thank goodness some of us can.' "

Then, too, certain models feel compelled to prove that they are not mentally deficient. Ed Fry says, "I find myself occasionally putting myself out to people a little farther than I may have normally simply to let them know that, no, I am not stupid, I am not an idiot. I may have cheekbones, but I am like anybody else, folks. Each individual has many facets. Just because somebody sells insurance doesn't mean he is incapable of doing anything else. Just because someone is a model doesn't mean he can't be interested in politics or have some type of social consciousness or maybe a consumer axe to grind. I do find myself

on the defensive, so I seem to spend a little more time letting people know, no, I am not a dumb blond. I am not even blond." Point of fact, Fry's hair is dark brown, and he does have cheekbones.

But strangers aren't the only people with fixed ideas. In numerous instances, parents cannot accept their model sons' profession.

"Oh, my family doesn't know what, how to feel, because my family is a very *bourgeois* French family," explains Loíc Raout, pronouncing the French word more precisely than the English. "They still think, you know, modeling is not a job for a man. I was to be an engineer."

Fred Souza, who felt incapable of coping with modeling in New York before traveling to France to become that country's most visible model

Fred Souza
Photo: Barry McKinley

in the late seventies, says, "My family is very New England. They still don't understand what I am doing. They keep asking when I am going to take a job. No matter how much money I make, still to them this is a very frivolous thing to do. Though I make more money than my father. It's hard. I have been in about five spreads in French *Vogue*, one completely by myself. And also a spread in *Elle*, a five-page spread, all by myself again, which is remarkable in a woman's magazine. I sent these to my parents, thinking they would be very excited. My mother works for a bank. I put some money into the bank. Her bank. After seeing all these things, they asked me when I was going to get a job."

"When I started, I really didn't understand the business, I didn't think it was a business. My father certainly didn't think of it as one," recalls Bill Carrico, speaking in the muted tones reserved for familial misunderstandings. "I was raised in Indianapolis and southern Indiana on my uncle's farm. It was drummed into us to get an education. Do this, that, and the other thing. I was going to be a marine biologist. It never dawned on me that money could be made without working for the other guy. My father didn't see any future in modeling. I would come home and he'd say, 'Well, that's nice. So-and-so has a job doing such-and-such, you ought to go out and try it.' 'Dad, I'm working, I'm doing all right.' He worked for the railroad, and men at work would ask him what I did. He didn't want to tell them I was a model. He told them I was doing TV commercials. I was just starting to make good money, maybe twenty-five thousand dollars a year, when my father died. He never believed I had a job."

Many models see their livelihood as quixotic and any gains as flukes. Then, at some unpredictable moment, something happens. In Loíc Raout's concise understatement, "I never thought I was such a great model until I realized I was very successful."

Some models have given up. Certain others, fewer in number, have caught on. The plodding over, they now have a strong foothold in a career of shifting sand.

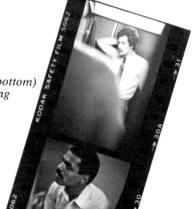

Two contact sheet frames—(top) Mark Shapiro; (bottom) Renauld White—taken in the dressing rooms during a Macy's fashion show. Photo: Peter Sakas

breezing along

After doing the *Merv Griffin Show*, I would have waiters or stewardesses come up and say, "Oh, I saw you on television," and shake my hand. It felt good. I did find that I began to be a little more conservative in my behavior. I realized that people watch TV and that they remember. They remember you more from a television appearance than from all your pictures put together. So I became a little more conservative. My behavior has not always been as upscale as it could be.

But the more important outcome of doing that show was that I had to get over my fear of not being safe anymore. Because that's what it means when you know you've almost reached your top in the field. Because where do you go from here? You have to put your ass on the line and start thinking of where you're going. It's a little scary if your credentials are knowing how to wear clothes and how to make a still photograph happen. Those credentials can take you nowhere. Except to another picture. So it's a scary period in a man's life.

I felt a new urgency. In 1978, I made a little bit more than fifty thousand dollars with television. But my average is not nearly what the top models in New York make. Because I was basically an L.A. model. I can make more than that, and will, now that I have chosen to live in New York again. But I haven't invested money wisely. I'm aware of it and I'm savin' me pennies now to invest, because I want that freedom. But male models are at a new point today. There are a lot of models like myself who have been around for ten or fifteen years. Before us, there wasn't a profession called male modeling. Men would dabble in it for

several years and get out or else they always had another job to go
to. Those guys didn't really have to think about what they were going to
do, because modeling wasn't all that serious. It didn't really take up
their lives. But now that men can make a great deal of money, those of
us who've been at it for a while wonder how long we can go on. I'm
curious how we're going to evolve from modeling into other fields. I hope
we do it gracefully.

I'm also curious about the guys who are just starting out. There will
always be new men coming in because this business is always looking for

exciting new faces. I don't resent it and I can even be intrigued by it.
I wonder what their intentions are beyond their hotshot flash. Because
persistence and determination count in building a career out of an
initial flash.

I don't know how many of the new guys have the guts to make it.
It ain't easy. There is a satisfaction in knowing that you're appreciated by
the rest of the world—or part of the rest of the world—simply for your
physical presentation. It can also make you neurotic. So we're talking
about a touchy sword with two edges, and there's a dangerous side to the
blade. But modeling doesn't have to be destructive. Not at all.

Models take drugs, of course. We're living in a drug generation. Let's
not pretend models don't take drugs. They do. How appropriately
depends on the model. I never take drugs the night before I work or
while I'm working. I have tried to work with drugs. I tried grass, except
I couldn't find the camera. I didn't care much. I tried cocaine and
modeling, except I couldn't stand still long enough to be photographed.
I worked on an up once because I was absolutely exhausted. I traveled
in from California to do a shooting for Camel cigarettes. I'd worked
all day prior in California. I took an up. I was supposed to be laughing
but I looked hysterical. My eyes were popping out of my head, my
smile was from one ear to the other. I was this hysterical person puffing
on a cigarette. I know models who need to take half a five-milligram
Valium to work with certain photographers. I would fall over the camera
and knock the photographer down.

Sure, I know of some models who have worked stoned and have done
just fine. But I have never known drugs to enhance a model's work. I
have seen models fuck up because of it. For the most part, drugs and
modeling are a stupid combination.

There are phases of drugs. When a new drug hits America, models
will be among the first to try it. Models are pretty hip people in that they
live three months in the future, at least in fashion, and probably in
most new trends, so once a drug hits, models are likely to be among the
first to know about it. So models play with a new drug before the rest
of the country does. I also think models yak it up a little just to prove
they're on top of it. They've lost a lot of money on expensive drugs like
cocaine. But then, who hasn't? From Wall Street to Spokane.

Drugs aren't the hard thing. Coming to terms with yourself can be.
You have to become responsible. You have to become grown up enough
to acknowledge what you've produced. I finally calmed down and
admitted I'd achieved something that looked like success. In a sense,
that was exciting. It was also a letdown. I began looking for other things.
Like this book. For a while it seemed there was less pleasure in what

This image was shot before the photographer,
and later Taylor, relocated to New York. Photo:
Albert Watson. Original printed in sepia.

I was doing. I thought, Oh, I'm just doing the same tired thing one more time. One day during a shooting I realized now is the time when I can really start making modeling absolutely fun. By being on a shooting and doing more than I normally would. By diverting my energy to succeed into energy directed to the job. By being a little more daring than I would before. By savoring the job. Not that you always can.

One of the big frustrations and dissatisfactions in this business is that people, particularly clients, constantly settle for less. Less than what the model has to give and less than what the photographer can ultimately see. So many clients feel: Crank it out, let's get it over and done with. That lessens the model and his talent. It lessens the photographer. Let me be a part of something great. I don't want to be mundane. I want things to be different because I've been around.

I've always been very particular about pictures. I'm not concerned about the way I look in person. That suits me fine. In pictures, I am more uncomfortable about the way I look. There are beautiful pictures of me, but I am not one of those models who never takes a bad picture. I do take a bad picture. So I work that much harder. But sometimes the cards are stacked against you.

One thing you learn as a model is that there will be some pictures that you hate. But I doubt that any model has ever hated a picture as much

as I hated this particular one of me—a double-page spread, right smack in the center of *GQ*. Taken inside a Braniff airplane. Me alone. In the middle aisle. Now the seats in this Braniff airplane were red, bright red, so when the film came back I looked as though I had scarlet fever. Well, the art director—dear Brian—said, "Oh, no problem. We'll do a dye transfer and it'll turn out beautiful." Well, it did. It turned out a beautiful shade of yellow. So now I looked like I had hepatitis. Except in the process of catching hepatitis, I lost all my features. So the art director once again said, "No problem, we'll just draw the features in." Well, I don't know what I had done to Brian but I ended up, double-page spread, looking like a hepatitic pig.

I do not have great luck with airplanes. I was doing a trip for Neiman-Marcus, my favorite client, to Amsterdam, and I was just thrilled. I flew from Los Angeles to meet the crew in Dallas, whereupon we waited for approximately four hours before taking off for Amsterdam. I can't sleep in planes, so I'm awake on this ten-hour flight from Dallas to Amsterdam. We get to Amsterdam, go through customs, check into our hotel. We are all exhausted, ready for bed. No bed. We have to turn around and go right back to the airport to do a shot of an airplane. Because of the trade agreement, we could only shoot this one plane, KLM or QUH, and we could only shoot it that day. It is summer. It is sticky hot. And we proceed to sit in a van for four more hours until they get this plane clear. Then, because it's the Neiman-Marcus Christmas book, I have to put on a woolen suit and a heavy coat. After about six hours sweltering, the shot is over and we head back into Amsterdam. I was feeling real weak, but I figured, what with no sleep, no food, it was natural I should feel a little weird and look a little green. Finally I got two hours of sleep and got up so sick the next day that I didn't know what hit me. We called a doctor. He didn't know either. He gave me a pill to relieve the chills and fever, which it didn't. What do you do when you're sick in Amsterdam when you're on a six-day booking? What I did was stay sick. And I would work. I would turn the garments wringing wet in the process of the shot. Someone would stand on the side with a towel, wiping me off until the shot was done. They took care of me and I took care of them. It was an unspoken agreement. They weren't cruel. I was there to work, and work I did. The minute the shot was over, I'd lie down and I'd fall instantly to sleep. When it was time for the next shot, they would prop me up. They would put me in a tuxedo and hand me a watch I was supposed to be looking at intently. I would look at the watch and drip into the watch until we got the shot. They would lay me back down and wake me up for the next shot.

On a location shooting with Mary Macuikas,
being photographed by Les Goldberg.

The shots didn't look as bad as I felt. I did look a little out of focus in some of them.

However, for my next job with Neiman-Marcus, they hired a private Lear jet. And we flew to Antigua. On the jet it was just our group. We played cards and we had our lunch and we had all the drinks in the world and good company. Great company. We partied on our Lear jet all the way to Antigua, where we landed, were met by limousines and were driven to the other side of this tropical island. In the harbor sat a 112-foot yacht, which we were motored out to. We spent our next six days in passage from one port to another. The island was ours. We had a French chef serving our meals. I had only three shots a day. For six days. If that isn't glamor, I don't know what is. We took our Lear jet back to Dallas. And I flew home to Los Angeles, suntanned and $3,700 richer.

Working with glamorous women is simply that. Glamorous. To work with the gorgeousness of a Renée Russo is a pleasure. It's a wonderful dance called Let's Take This Picture. You enhance each other. And to have that beauty draped on your arm or leaning against your shoulders, it's just a pleasure. The biggest diamonds, the biggest furs, the biggest eyes, the most hair, the prettiest tits, the smallest waist, give me that. I love it.

One of the most beautiful shootings I did was for *Harper's Bazaar.* I was to be the backup for Cheryl Tiegs. We shot at Big Sur, riding horses, backpacking, fishing in rivers. We stayed in a beautiful lodge hanging on the side of Big Sur overlooking the surf, with hot whirlpool baths, a big Olympic swimming pool, private rooms. I had not worked with Cheryl before and I was a little apprehensive. This lady's a big star. I wanted it to work between us. If it doesn't work, what are you going to do for six days, apologize? Hate it? Cheryl was a little cool initially. But it took us only until the afternoon for her to realize we were *sympatico.* We got on great. She allowed me to prop her, to make her laugh. She's a very beautiful woman and a hard worker. In rain and fog, she is a professional. She will do anything necessary for the shot. Which inspired me to do anything to have it work. Now, I was cut out of all but two of the pictures. That's okay. Given *Harper's,* that happens. The same with *Vogue.* But it was a pleasure to work with one of the world's most successful and beautiful women.

I'd have to be a real creep to complain about my work in California. It was great. After I left New York, I didn't come back to New York for four years. After the Griffin show, though, I knew I had to come back. I'd have to make a commitment to stay, to be the top of whatever

This Revlon International ad with Renée Russo appeared
in Europe but not in the U.S. Photo: Richard Noble

it is I'm going to be the top of. I wanted some of the good work that only New York has to offer. I wanted some good editorial. I wanted some good national ads. So I came back. To savor the business. To perfect the craft. And also to plan for something new.

It's been a joy, just a joy. I love working with beautiful women and men. The other day I had a booking I dreaded. It was shooting a catalog for big ladies. And they were *big ladies*. It's the only shooting I've ever been on when I've heard clients say, "Oh my God, Agnes, you're getting thin. You must have milk shakes at lunch. Here, have some cheesecake." I was the prop for these ladies, their background. Because I'm six/three —too tall for the business—I was chosen to go with these big ladies. I was sitting at the piano, pounding away at nothing, singing anything that came into my mind. I sang: "Isn't it beautiful the way I sing; aren't we having a wonderful time; get this shot done, this is a turkey; help, help, help, get me out of here." The ladies were great. They were going for their angles just like Renée and Cheryl. And they were beautiful. They relied on me to create an atmosphere where they could laugh and have fun and go for their angles, which were more round than angular. By the end of the day, we had a very feisty little group. Given willing people, you can turn almost any shooting into a fun day, a day that you can't legitimately call work.

Right now, I have options. I could drop modeling and really go for

the acting. I could do many other things and not be afraid to live. But I want to savor this business before I move on. Sure, my acting career has suffered because of modeling. And I don't give a damn. I wasn't ready to act. I'll be a much better actor at this point than I would have been at twenty-five. I don't think it will be harder at thirty-five. If I'd really wanted acting then, I'd have gone and got it. I think it will be easier now, given who I am now as opposed to who I was then. I think I'm far more simply a man now. In fact, I may end up selling shoes at Macy's. Except I don't think I will, given who I am. I'll be fine. Period.

—M.T.

Once upon a time, professional male models were Real People. To themselves, they never cease being so. While a model is struggling, most people grant him Real Person status precisely because he hasn't made it yet and could still fall flat on his face. Empathizing with his efforts is easy; common folks try to beat the system in their own way every day of their lives. Should the aspiring model triumph against the odds, however, he transcends their experience: his Real Person status is rescinded. He becomes the mythic Male Model.

At this plateau, the model goes through some contradictory emotions himself. With unconscious irony, he adopts the prevailing jargon of outsiders and refers to his off-camera hours as his "real life." How deep this self-alienation goes depends upon the individual's emotional makeup. He may chuckle at the comedic aspects of his situation; he may rail against his condition. Usually his reaction is a combination of these two extremes. He has ambivalences of his own. He loves the money but hates having to manage it. Or, he loves the freedom but doesn't know how to fill his free time. Or, he loves the travel but resents never being able to plan a vacation of his own.

Contradictions are piled upon contradictions, with one central dichotomy. Although he may never have verbalized it, one of the motivations that propelled him toward his career in the first place was a wish to be admired for his physicality. To a large degree, that wish is now fulfilled. He knows he wouldn't be where he is today without his looks. But getting what he wanted may not feel so hot. What about the *real* him? At this juncture, the model wants to be seen as more than the sum of his physical parts. He wants his humanity back, something both his idolators and his detractors don't want to return. Usually he looks upon his perverse dilemma as kind of a joke. Seldom drowning in tears, he generally feels his life is fine, except it would be finer still

Assessing his modeling career and acting opportunities, Taylor says, "Sure, my acting career has suffered because of modeling. And I don't give a damn." Photo: Loíc Raout

if he were allowed to emerge as an individual. He may exult in his accomplishments, but his joy is laced with a hint of melancholy.

Other changes occur once a model's career shifts into high gear. Although the business remains as unpredictable as ever, the successful model realizes he has arrived. Rationally, he knows that his career could skid to a screeching halt the very next day. But he knows at gut level that it won't. He has a new confidence. Not that he has no insecurities. He may worry about aging. He may still feel personally rejected when a go-see doesn't pan out. He may look at up-and-comers and wonder if they'll surpass him. He can feel complacent or arrogant or hollow. However he feels at this point, he feels *different*. And he is. If success is sweet or sour, only a fraction of male models ever taste it.

Almost immediately after realizing he has made the grade, the model asks himself a question: What will I do when I stop modeling? Prior to the recognition that he has indeed arrived, the model's vision tended to be shortsighted. Most of his energies were spent on achieving success. Success attained, he now takes a long-range view. And the scene can be chilling. Will he be one of the lucky guys who model into their forties or, rarer still, into their fifties? He can't count on it. He'd better make some plans. *What* plans?

With nearly thirty-five years in the business, Bill Loock has watched scores of men enter and leave modeling. If breaking in is difficult, exiting gracefully is not much easier. "The average guy today is a lot more aware of the need to plan ahead," he says. "And guys today can make so much money in a short time. But getting out must be a little devastating, a downer. It's difficult to prepare yourself to walk away from modeling. You almost have to start a business of your own, like a restaurant. You're so spoiled from a money standpoint. And your modeling experience isn't worth much if you haven't worked at something else. You're spoiled for other things. Because modeling really is a glamorous business. There's a lot of nitty-gritty, but there's a helluva lot that's glamorous. You work with a lot of handsome people. If they're not handsome, they're interesting. I've been to Europe so many times. Australia, Japan, all the islands, all the main cities in this country. And when I got there, I didn't need to worry about where I'd eat or where I'd sleep."

Aware that the bucks are big but the time spans can be short, the top-echelon model wants to relish his success—and usually does—but the future is always gnawing at the present.

Keith Gog is in his early thirties and for nearly a decade has been the epitome of "juvenile," the industry term for a model of slightly smaller stature or younger appearance who represents the wholesome, well-scrubbed, All-American teen or young-man image. Gog began modeling while he was an industrial design student. "I started part time, then modeling overpowered the schooling. I liked the money. The

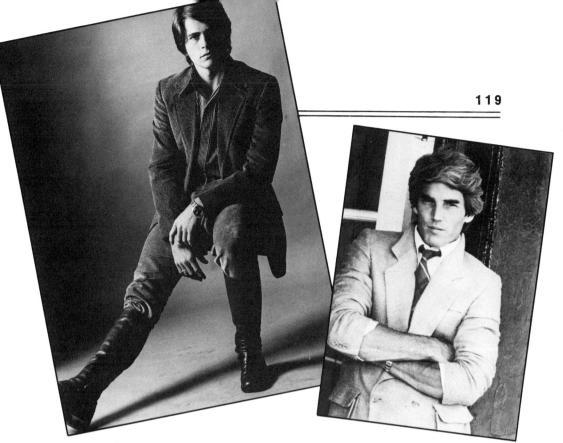

monopoly money, as I call it. Play money. I made it in a hurry and I spent it in a hurry. People were always saying I should invest in something. And I did. I have gone into two business ventures. I opened up a clothing store and I had a discotheque. And I used the money to support an art addiction. Plus travel. When someone says, 'Where is your money?' I think about it and realize that it has all been spent and a lot of it has been spent on total fun. I could never put a price on that. Some people get into more material, solid possessions—accumulated wealth. Travel is intangible. You can't store it anywhere but in the mind.

"In the beginning, I was going to retire at twenty-six and have my own art studio," Gog recalls. "I thought maybe I could have a hundred thousand cash and I could build my studio in the country and buy all my equipment. As it stands, I am not retired. And I don't know when I will. I did finally build my own little studio, but it is not in the country. There have been these compromises and I am nowhere near being able to just do what I would like to do."

In fact, most male models haven't a clue to what they ultimately "want to do." Well over half think an acting career would be just dandy, and a large percentage do study acting, though acting is as unpredictable as modeling. Here and there, a model starting out may study architecture or law, but most models are very unspecific about planning for retirement. Once the money starts accumulating, the more practical-minded put it to work as a cushion against a future with no guarantees.

During 1978, Scott MacKenzie had three exclusive contracts, almost unheard of in male modeling. One was with Gant Shirtmakers, another

Keith Gog (left) perennial junior. Photo: Ken Haak.
Scott MacKenzie, "workaholic." Photo: Gary Bernstein

with formal-wear manufacturer Palm Beach, the third with Hastings, a clothing store in San Francisco. "I like the contracts because I don't have to work that hard," MacKenzie says. "Let's say for Gant and Palm Beach, for each I work four days in December and four days in June or July. For Hastings I also work eight days a year. Each client pays me a certain amount—not a large amount, but it is comfortable—each month to guarantee that I will not work for competitors. With Gant, I can't do anybody else's national shirt ad. With Palm Beach, no other ads for tuxedos. With Hastings, no other billboard that would appear in San Francisco. But I can do all the catalogs and noncompetitive products such as hair blowers, shaving products, soaps."

MacKenzie describes himself as "a workaholic" and is among the top-grossing models in the United States. Still, "If someone said to me right now, 'Stop, you have to quit,' I would say, 'Gee, what am I going to do in order to afford what I have now?' This business can be a trap," he remarks. "It traps you a bit financially. I have never lived above my means, but it is frightening at times. Because at twenty-nine to have what I have, I could never have gotten it until I was thirty-nine on a regular type of job. What happens at thirty-nine? Success in this business is not how much you work but what you do with your money," Mac-Kenzie declares.

"I think one of the most tragic things is to see someone who has been on top in this business and who has blown his whole wad," says Greg Bauer. "When the party lights go out, it is really sad to see. I've been investing in property. I've bought a condominium in Hawaii and my brother Bruce and I just bought some property together in Idaho. Everybody keeps asking, 'What are you going to do when you finish modeling?' They make it sound like the end of the world is coming: What are you going to do when your face drops to your ankles? I don't exactly know at this moment what I'll do. But I know that with the money I'm making, by investing it wisely, I'm sort of covered."

"I have invested just about everything I have made," says Tony Spinelli, who has modeled for eight years. "Common sense tells me good things don't last forever, nothing does. I have government bonds. I'm involved in the stock market. But not as much as I'm involved in real estate. I own my apartment and I also have a house in the country. A minifarm. Fifteen acres. And I own another condominium."

Real estate heads the list of model investments. Bill Carrico has become involved in purchasing and renovating apartment buildings in Chicago. But he has other business interests as well: "I have a small corporation I formed. We design and manufacture sterling silver giftware. I am in partnership with another company, Argento Enterprises, which is a large corporation that makes about nine hundred and fifty pieces of jewelry and even some leather handbags. Most of it is made in Italy. I use their manufacturing facilities to make my designs. The main thing I am selling right now is a silver joint case. No one else has put those out in a very elegant form. A case simply designed for joints, that's it. We are selling them in the best stores in the country, and they retail at about two hundred dollars.

"I'd like to retire within five years. If I could retire by the time I am forty, that would be terrific. I just want to get a farm and settle back, have friends out, race motorcycles. Nothing is more valuable to me than play time," Carrico says. "It would be nice to be a millionaire, but I'm not sure that it might not be more work than it is worth."

"I have a little money into stock," relates Joe MacDonald, "but mostly I have bought photographs. That's what interests me most right now. I started just buying individual pictures that I liked. Now I'm really excited. This spring, starting in Seattle, fifty-five of my photographs will be shown in museums. They will be gone for two years. A two-year show to end up here in New York, in Brooklyn at the Brooklyn Museum. Some of my favorites are Man Ray and Steichen. And then some newer people like Skrebneski. I have some Avedons. I have some Scavullos. Guy Bourdin. Helmut Newton. Horst. All different stuff. I realized that photography is really the art form of the twentieth century and that any museum or art collector would eventually have to recognize photography as the modern art form that it is."

Because male modeling has solidified as a serious career only in the past several years, today's professionals don't have role models against which to pattern their transition back into "real life." Previously, few men supported themselves exclusively by modeling, and the money they earned was in no way comparable to current rewards. Of the business demigods, Bill Loock never gave up the security of the insurance business and Ted Dawson is still active in modeling. A number of thirtyish men approaching their forties who've never known a career other than modeling haven't had to decide yet what to do five or ten years hence. The top models today are truly the "first generation" professional. Twenty years ago there were no male model superstars because the profession wasn't even a real one. Today, men in their twenties can make upward of fifty grand a year. And they can be has-beens at thirty. How members of the profession as a whole will cope with this situation is yet to be seen. The successes and failures are too recent to be viewed dispassionately. That's why so many models today are intent on grabbing some form of long-range financial security: who knows what the future will bring? As Craig Vandenburgh, one of the world's top male models in the late 1960s, says, "The only thing that is really hard about modeling is that, unlike other professions where people go up, up, up, we go down, down, down. It is inevitable that we will be out on our asses. Inevitable and guaranteed. The minute you are at your peak, you are beginning to go down. No matter what you do, you can't stop it. It is like growing old. You can't stop it. You can delay it sometimes, but you can't stop it. And I think it is terrifying."

So, with their futures an uncertainty, many top models feel they must

Don Guide says he could "stand on top of a church steeple and do a job." Photo: Bill Carrico

further refine and perfect their craft in order to augment their bookings and to amass more money even faster. If they are not careful, their behavior can become compulsive. On the other hand, if they maintain their equilibrium while trying to earn more, they may learn more, hopefully uncovering new joys in the process.

Experience also yields confidence, so unusual sessions may not be as nerve-racking as they once were. "There are so many variables," notes Don Guide. "You go on a job and you think it's a studio job. Then the photographer takes you to Water Tower Place with three hundred people standing in a crowd watching you. There are people waving, girls winking, guys trying to make you laugh. Your whole mind was set for a studio shot, now there are three hundred people all looking at you. That is kind of crazy at first. Now, I could stand on top of a church steeple and do a job and it wouldn't bother me."

Working with some of the world's best photographers can make working with the mediocre less than exciting. But a model may reap pleasure from his greater knowledge of the technical aspects at hand. "I learned a lot about light and that whets my appetite to learn more," notes Kalani Durdan. "I am to the point where if the light is very bad, I will mention it to the photographer. Usually we can work it out. When I see a bad photograph of me, I think back to the day of the shooting, and try to figure out what went wrong. Maybe it was the lens the photographer was using. Or maybe it was me. I used to have a lot of bad pictures when I was heavier."

The longer someone models, the harder it can be for him to generate the old excitement. Brad Forrest modeled in New York, London, Europe and Los Angeles before migrating, at the suggestion of agent Nina Blanchard, to Chicago. "It's not as much fun as it used to be," he allows. "Modeling today is very competitive. I still enjoy what I do. I enjoy it because I'm a different character every day. One day I'm a daddy with a bunch of kids. One day I'm a businessman behind the desk. It isn't the same routine every day. After twenty-two years in this business, I couldn't sit behind a desk, nine to five, five days a week, for anything. That part of it is still fun for me. But as far as it *really* being fun? It's fun when you are young and have great ambitions. It is not fun anymore like it used to be. It is dollars and cents for me now. It is a way to make a lot of money without sitting behind a desk nine to five."

Ted Dawson also hates the idea of a desk job, but doesn't fret when every day isn't earthshaking. "It's a business, and basically it's a glamorous business," he maintains. "You work X amount of hours a day and that's it. You go to the Caribbean in the winter on business. I don't mind standing there with a couple of pins up my ass, I really don't. At least I'm standing in the sun. I'm not sitting behind a desk."

But as far as having enthusiasm for the actual work of posing, by the time a model is breezing along, there's usually less electricity in the air. "I no longer have a specific goal in modeling," admits Randall Lawrence. "I used to want to do more creative work, but after a while I transferred my interest to the people involved in the shooting, not the shooting itself. I can do an everyday catalog as happily as a *Vogue* shooting. It isn't the actual photograph that absorbs me. It is the people I work with. Then a fairly boring modeling job, a fairly boring picture, can become interesting."

Denis La Marsh echoes Lawrence's sentiments. "Modeling has become extremely mechanical. I know what I have to do. I do it. I get the voucher signed and I leave. It is not fun. Not now. Unless I'm working with buddies and good-time people and the situation is light and easy. Then it is practically relaxing. Otherwise, I give pose one through forty-six and that's it. Because the exploration of yourself and what you can create is gone. It is all pat at this point."

Though some models prefer rediscovering the sense of anticipation and sense of adventure they felt when starting out, many photographers believe that the longer models pursue their craft, the better their performance. "The best models work the hardest," says Les Goldberg. "The top guys are the easiest to get along with, the most professional, the least arrogant. What makes the peaks is everybody's energy level. Everybody wanting to make a photograph wonderful. To make it better. If there's a way to make the shot better despite the god-awful things going against you, that's the biggest challenge. I did a shot with Randall Lawrence in a blizzard with hundred-and-twenty-five-mile-an-hour winds. Randall was walking into the snow and you could barely see him, the snow was so thick. His willingness to go out in that and to take a chance to make a great photograph was wonderful. The van got stuck in the mud. We were all filthy and cold and wet and tired. We traveled a thousand miles in four days through four states in the worst weather conditions. In a situation like that—even the van driver was a pain in the ass—when everybody's behind you and nobody's complaining and everybody's into the shooting, that's brilliance. When people are willing to give that kind of energy, that's when you hit the peak."

Models, riding high professionally, often begin to view themselves in a more detached manner. "In some ways, modeling is like a one-way mirror," says Ed Fry. "The glamor is attractive and exciting and compelling, the magic that comes out on the printed page. Not only is that

compelling for the buying public, it is compelling for the model. And yet, as I model, I see both sides. I see all the pins and the tape on the back of the clothing. So, in another way, modeling is a two-way mirror for the model. And then modeling loses its glamor."

And since many models feel they must dig in and work harder to mine the riches while they can, large numbers feel their positions are not less, but more, precarious the higher they ascend. "Once you've hit the top, it's rougher," evaluates Jon Gilmore earnestly, brushing his blond hair off his forehead. "It was much easier coming up. A model is like a bird in flight. Once you are up there, you are winging it. You have to stay in the air constantly. Your wings get tired."

If modeling itself becomes less rewarding in terms of personal satisfaction, the model often turns to his "real life" for special rewards. But the fact that he's a model sometimes gets in the way. Jon Gilmore continues: "We are illusion. Models are illusion. When I am walking down the street or I am in a bar, people still identify me as an illusion. To them, I am not real. I do not look like them, and that's why I'm a model. After ten years in the business, I can't help but strike a pose. I don't intend to do it, but I will sit a certain way. I look calm if I'm nervous. Standing at a bar, I still look like a mannequin. Sometimes I just psych myself out. I can actually see my face, you know, as if I'm pointing a camera at myself. I am standing there, and because of my experience, I can actually see my own face and my expression in my mind. And that just psychs me out."

Unable to escape being models, some guys try to get their personal kicks from the fact that they are. One gay model relates, "I know there

Ed Fry says, "Modeling is a two-way mirror for the model." Photos: Peter Ogilvie

was a period in my life when I got laid solely out of being a model. A lot of guys weren't even attracted to my type but went home with me anyway, just so they could go back to the bar and say, 'I had him. He's not that great. He's a lousy lay.' I know how people are. I could never have gotten those fuckers in bed if I hadn't been in *Playboy* magazine for twenty pages. 'He looks like shit in real life.' I got a lot more sex after I started modeling for the very reason that I was a model."

Of course, resentments can creep in when the model, solely because he is a model, is awarded indiscriminate special treatment. "You know the way a sexy blond hates the way men treat her?" Randall Lawrence asks. "Well, that's the way I hate being treated by women. And it happens a lot. Being fawned over is not an easy thing to deal with. I don't like it when people only relate to me physically. It's frustrating. Or say you're shooting on the street. People walk by and make comments. 'Oh, get him.' The comments are usually along sexual lines. That you're not a man. Sometimes I answer, 'If you were making as much money as I, you'd be doing this too, but you're too damned ugly.' Not often, but sometimes the urge is irresistible.'"

Telling a model how fortunate he is is an almost foolproof way of raising his ire. "A lot of lay people think all a model does is stand in front of a camera and smile," says Bruce Bauer, his frown pinching his eyebrows. "What pisses me off is when I hear, 'Aren't you lucky to be in this business?' Luck didn't have a goddamn thing to do with it. I worked my ass off to get where I am today."

But unless those lay people are very close to the model, they never truly understand all the ramifications of his professional milieu and its emotional demands. Even when an outsider is closely related, odds are that he still will have a distorted view of the model's world and life. "My father is hysterical," says Kalani Durdan, laughing heartily. "He still thinks I'm doing a summer job that has lasted several years."

Because it is extremely difficult to communicate the exact nature of their profession, and because the nature of the work is repetitive, models often talk in generalities about their rewards. They extol Money; they laud Freedom; they commend Creative People; they praise Travel. But they often do so in a peculiarly self-deprecating manner. It has become unfashionable for models to mention Glamor—emphasizing Hard Work is *de rigueur* these days. With their newfound but shaky professional status, many male models feel they must, in keeping with the Protestant work ethic, sublimate their joys and make solemn statements about being only "salesmen." Well, mere salesmen rarely have such luxurious fringe benefits. And models know it. Again, models are in a contradictory position. If they gloat about glamor, they're accused of being superficial. (If a factory worker fell into the model's circumstances, he would be expected to brag. In fact, if he didn't, he'd be berated for not sharing his adventures for the vicarious enjoyment of his friends.) But if they downplay the glamor in favor of the mundane, models are accused of dishonesty. (If the factory worker doesn't complain about tedium, he isn't one of the gang.)

Given the choice, almost anyone would select the model's job over the factory worker's. If both occupations have elements of hard work, the factory worker seldom partakes of the glamor afforded the model. The flash of their eyes and the width of their smiles when models relate their favored moments prove they have their special compensations.

"I like being on vacation all year long," is the way Loíc Raout describes a model's life. Travel is the plus most top models single out.

Ted Dawson: "I've done weird things. I've climbed to the top of the pyramids and I've been photographed up there from a helicopter. I've been on a raft in the middle of the Thames when the female model fell right into the river. There she was, dripping wet, holding this big false eyelash in her fingers. Everybody started to clap. She was smiling. It was fabulous. Most models are taken places where tourists don't go. In Bangkok, we went to the palace and saw incredible things no tourist has ever seen."

Keith Gog: "The doors that travel opens are the intangibles. I did a trip for Avon and there was this one guy, me, and three really beautiful women, the kind that guys in America grow up dreaming about. It is like you live a fantasy. Only you really *live* it. Dropping in on Paris. Eating at a little café. Being there with some gorgeous Swedish model. If they set up a movie set, they couldn't make it any more beautiful. And you are the main character. Those kinds of enjoyment in this business are priceless."

Fred Souza: "I spent a week in the Indian Ocean doing a few pictures. I spent ten days on the Arctic coast. I've seen sunsets in the Alps. I've fallen asleep on a train from the French Alps and woken on the Riviera to see the Mediterranean on one side and the red cliffs of France on the other. I've spent the morning watching the sun come up on the Acropolis. I did a job for English *Vogue* in Scotland. We stayed in the manor house of a man who was one of Darwin's best friends. The castle was on a loch fed by the Gulf Stream. Tropical plants could grow there. There were plants from all over the world. The gardens and landscape were remarkable. These things affect you."

Tony Spinelli: "One of the nicest trips I have ever had was for *Gentlemen's Quarterly*. Most of the shooting was done on the *Michelangelo*. We sailed from New York to Napoli. My mother happens to come from a town which is about an hour from Naples. It was a two-and-a-half-week trip. We traveled first class, ate first class, it was first class all the way. Once we arrived in Naples, we spent the next week in the country photographing. Then we went on to Capri. We were shooting in the center of Capri, in a piazza with all these cafés. There were at least two hundred people gathering around and watching the shooting. Dynamite. I love working outside in public. It was like a fashion show. They were my audience. I loved it. It brought more out of me."

Conrad Bell: "One year you're stuck in a blizzard in Chile, designing some furs, and one year later, to the day, you are asked to go to Russia for the same client—Neiman-Marcus—this time to model your own fur collection. Incredible. There I was on a Baltic cruise. Now that is a long way from the cotton patch in Georgia. I always knew there was something out there, but I didn't know that I would find it. In one way, it was not a pleasant trip. It was depressing. My bus was bugged. A taxi driver tried to rip me off. But it was beautiful. Leningrad was incredible. It was like Paris, except in pastel colors. Blues and pinks. But just the idea of going to the country and being on a Baltic cruise. And being paid for it. All because you were lucky enough to be born with a certain look. Anybody who takes that for granted and misuses it is an asshole."

Nonetheless, even travel can have its negatives.

Rob Yoh: "I've been to practically every island in the Caribbean. Europe a few times. Paris. Italy. London. Dubrovnik, which was wonderful. Germany I really didn't like. Twice in India. I have been to Japan three times. To Hong Kong. I think traveling is wonderful. *Except,* you're always leaving tomorrow. Bye-bye. You leave the home front, loved ones, family, apartment. The plumber is coming in two days, but you're leaving tomorrow. Nothing gets done."

Scott MacKenzie: "This was my travel schedule last month. Starting in New York, I flew to San Francisco. San Francisco to Los Angeles. Los Angeles to New York. Los Angeles again. To Puerto Rico. Puerto

Hard Work is emphasized over Glamor these days. Tony Spinelli (center) and Loíc Raout, joined by Apollonia (left) and Pat Cleveland. Hair & makeup by Ara Gallant. Styled by Giorgio St. Angelo. Photo: Barry McKinley

Rico to New York. New York to St. Croix. St. Croix to New York to Milan. Milan to New York. New York to Los Angeles again. Los Angeles to San Francisco to Los Angeles to New York. Over twenty-five thousand miles in four weeks, all connected to work. I have two different lives. I have one life in Los Angeles. A wife and child. A business in automobiles. Insurance policies, house payments, employees. Then I have modeling. In Los Angeles, I have a wife and a child whom I never see because of my schedule. It is like Dr. Jekyll and Mr. Hyde."

Jim Gibbs: "You feast or you famine. If you want to plan a trip for the period you're slow, you'll call the agency and book out. Within three hours they'll call and say, 'Two days from now you've got a booking you can't turn down.' I've had more vacations not happen."

For some models, travel takes a back seat to other rewards.

Joe MacDonald: "I defy someone to say that a booking with Dick Avedon isn't glamorous. Anyone would have to be blind and deaf. Seriously. There is a stimulation, a taste level, an atmosphere in his studio. Same thing at Scavullo's or at Skrebneski's or at Albert Watson's, or working with Chris von Wangenheim. Those photographers make you feel special. It is the whole atmosphere. Having beautiful girls around, beautifully dressed. People are what glamor is."

Craig Vandenburgh: "It has always made me feel good to be on a plane or in a restaurant and to have someone say, 'Haven't I seen your picture in a magazine, aren't you a model?' I don't feel like such an ant walking through the city. Modeling has a Russian roulette quality I have always loved about it. You may not work for a couple weeks and you get all scared, and then, Boom! you are going to Bermuda for a week. There is no easier way on God's earth to make money. You stand in front of a camera and are paid a fortune for nothing. I made a thousand dollars a couple weeks ago doing a Seagram's ad and the whole thing took about four hours. I was fed, I was pampered, I made people laugh. It was a day that was more fun than going to a party."

Partying, however, is a subject most models are not eager to discuss. Just as it is fashionable to emphasize hard work over glamor, it is vogue to discount the party circuit. This is another of the many contradictions in modeling. Large numbers of models party hard. They are seen boogieing at the New York disco Studio 54 (called simply "54" by habitués and readers of *Women's Wear Daily*), where gaining admission depends more on how you look than who you are. There is never a shortage of people lining up outside 54 hoping to pass inspection, and models inevitably win the nod: they're part of the lush scenery.

Middle-class members of the singles set are indulged in their fun-is-all philosophy because they are "gainfully employed" as office workers, teachers and junior executives. Models, though, defensively try to paint a picture of their lifestyle as consistent with the sober values of the middle class, precisely because they are regarded as outsiders who don't really "work" for a living. But what about the tales of easy sex and accessible drugs? Do models live model lives or are they a promiscuous, decadent bunch?

It is doubtful that models as a group lead any more amoral—or lonely—lives than the singles set. Individually, models range from goody two-shoes to gross debauchers. There are bar brawlers and teetotalers. There are faithful husbands and feckless philanderers. There are health nuts and pill poppers. There are virgins (few) and satyrs (also few).

Collectively, models are hard to characterize. Brian Burdine makes a good effort: "Models, like actors and actresses, are very competitive. That is a big plus for them, because they become more alive, have more on the ball. Most of them are incredibly attractive. Most are single, relatively young. Likes attract each other. They always seem to be with attractive people from other walks of life, such as writers and playwrights and people in film. Not just because of their looks. Models are basically fun. One might think that because they are the center of attention so much of the time, models would all be neurotic. I don't find that, I find that models have a lot of confidence, so in a social sense they are very lively. They handle their drugs incredibly. I can only think of two or three men whose careers have been ruined by drugs. Most models—at least the ones I know and like—have a lot of energy and are very upbeat people. They are very much the way they look. They are well traveled. They don't have to be anything. They don't have to be intellectual. They are usually good people, energetic and willing. What is most attractive is an innate sense of their own style. The ones who have hit the top have oftentimes done so not because they are attractive or photograph well, but because of their own particular style."

For more than a few, drugs are part of that style, usually not while working, but frequently during their "real life."

Nina Blanchard heaves a deep sigh before answering the question of whether drug and pill usage is widespread among models. "No," she insists, discharging a dense cloud of smoke. "In the sixties, drugs were rampant. Drug usage in the modeling world is no goddamn different than drug usage by nurses. It's worse with doctors. If you took a cross section of truck drivers, I bet you'd find just as many truck drivers on pills as models. We may get them first, because we're more chic, you know." She laughs, drawing out another cigarette. "If there's a new pill out, we're going to be the first to know about it. We know that coke is rampant in our industry. It's rampant. But it's not just the models, it's everybody else too. Directors, producers, writers. *And* insurance executives in Orange County. Models have a certain physical beauty. Along with that physical beauty goes the drama of tragedy people want to read about. The fact that a nineteen-year-old is on the cover of everything and then kills herself on drugs, that's more dramatic than the unattractive dental hygienist who OD's."

It may be that heightened contrast—beauty and its destruction—that makes Jon Gilmore's anecdote so horrifying. "Drugs are almost non-

existent in Chicago," he says. "The biggest drug is grass. Models are not on ups, they are not on downs. In New York—I'm being honest— a great percentage of models are snorting before jobs. I did a job with this chick once who will remain nameless. She was into drugs. I thought, no big deal. We all did it. But she was snorting it for a long time. If you do a gram of coke a week, eventually it is going to turn on you. We were shooting and her nose was running. She blew her nose. The photographer, who was standing behind the camera, said, 'What happened? What is wrong with your nose?' She had broken her nose."

Do models use more drugs than our increasingly drug-oriented society? Who can say? But the odds are that they do. They have the means and the access. Do they party more? Probably. At least at the beginning. As Zoli says, "Most models start at a relatively young age. Modeling is a youth market. Most models do not come from Manhattan. They arrive and they are in awe or they are impressed. And they're invited many places because they're attractive. There are lots of temptations. They think that this is all wonderful. Then they realize, 'Well, all I'm getting from this is very tired. My work is suffering. Enough.' Thank God they're young enough to recuperate. Some people, of course, don't realize what they're doing to themselves. They burn out."

Some have to leave New York to resist its temptations. Jon Gilmore settled for a more sane existence modeling in Chicago. "In New York, I think the great percentage of people involved in modeling are thieves and whores," Gilmore says. "I was. In the beginning, I would have cut my mother's throat for a job. I was there for three years. But the third year, I looked around and saw models growing older, doing the same shit, and I kept wondering: Do I want to turn forty in New York? As a blond, I felt like an endangered species. Anything you want, if it isn't in New York, it doesn't exist. If a model wasn't working Tuesday, he'd call you Monday night to go boogie. And you had male stylists working for a magazine, pulling down a hundred and twenty a week and having all this incredible power. They'd wear models around them like jewelry. New York was exciting as hell. But you can't burn that fast."

Jon Gilmore (above). With Cynthia Newhouse. Photo: Izokaitis.
Blowing bubbles. Photo: Rick Mitchell. (Opposite) David White
says, "You have to come back to earth before you can leave
again." Photo: Barry McKinley

Although numbers of models run fast, when the running becomes wearying, most have the sense to carve a quiet niche for themselves. Some may continue to stumble stoned on Fire Island or to punch it out in public, but the majority, having sown their oats, reap some restful solitude.

David White's brilliant blue eyes—he was the cover model for *GQ*'s "blue" issue—have a private cast when he discusses how he spends his off-duty hours. "I like to be able to lock my door and forget about everything. I like to lie around and listen to country music. When you go out, all you hear is disco music. That's fine while you're out. But when you go home by yourself, you don't want music that shocks your nerves. You have to come back to earth before you can leave again. I collect porcelains. Bums. I am a freak on bums. Maybe I think one day I am

Then and now. Randall Lawrence. Early photo: Barry McKinley. Portrait: Bruce Weber. Renauld White. First composite: Charles Tracy. Head shot: Michael O'Brien. Bill Loock. Current: Erik McKenzie

going to end up a bum. I have always had this thing in the back of my head. So I collect books on bums. Pictures of bums. Porcelain bums. Mentally, I talk to my men. My apartment looks like a log cabin. It is my own little world."

Wherever models locate their private refuges, the public world of modeling spins with its own revolutions. As images change in advertising, models go through phases of popularity. To hold their lead, established models must adapt, to some degree, to popular tastes. As Brian Burdine explains, "Fashion is like the automobile industry. Clothing has to become obsolete. If styles change, then models who represent fashion trends must also change. When I was first at *GQ*, the rage for models was smoldering European. Now advertising is into very healthy, very active sporty types of men. There isn't one overall look, of course, but one look will prevail at any particular time and will influence the other looks. There's still a European look, but it's less smoldering."

As male advertising and editorial images shift, the models most affected are those the industry calls "exotic" types, the men with very out-of-the-ordinary faces that command attention because of their uniqueness. Being of Japanese ancestry, Les Hamaguchi is in the exotic category. "When I first talked to Wilhelmina, she said she wouldn't lead me on," Hamaguchi remarks. "She made it very clear that I wouldn't work every day. And I haven't. I worked more during the first two years because of the packaging of the product. I did much more then because I found the time to do more. As my responsibilities in advertising grew, I had less time. But the demand for using me has also lessened. In the initial stages, I went around and saw a lot of photographers and just got to be known because I was the only Oriental or whatever. I don't have to go out and do a lot of selling now: I am known to exist, and if people want to use me, they will. I still do a lot of live shows. But I could not live on modeling. If I were seen as often as Ted Dawson the wearout factor would be much greater for me."

Denis La Marsh has a very distinctive look and manages to work steadily. However, he has opened a florist business, Perry Water in New York City, just in case. "It gets to be very snug and easy at a certain point, and then suddenly there is a new group of models who are being booked," La Marsh says. "So you have to work a little bit harder. You have to make sure your contacts are still good and that you are well liked. Modeling is a fickle business. One year you are in, the next year you are out. And the following year you are back in again. I can be working my ass off at certain times when certain guys are not working at all. Only because there aren't a lot of people around with the same look I have. At present, I seem to have the graying, balding-with-a-beard market cornered. I can't believe no one has knocked off my look. I have seen people try it, but they have fallen short."

Even men who are more conventionally handsome have to update themselves and their approaches to fashion. After fifteen years in the business, Ken Baker still works in Europe for a month every year. "It's very important for my book to change every year, and it's important for me to keep up with European trends. As a man gets older, the work becomes more limited, which makes it even more important to keep on your toes. I love the business so much, and I thought if I wanted to stay in the industry, I had to concentrate on areas other than print. I concentrated on television. Currently I have eight or nine national commercials on the air. During the last five years, my television earnings have increased in such a way that I am still earning the same money—more money, in fact—than I was earning ten years ago when I was working around the clock. I shifted gears."

Although he started modeling in 1957, Brad Forrest still experiments with new tactics to keep himself fresh in clients' eyes. "I put out a comp once a year, and I have always felt that is the best way," he notes. "I got the idea of doing a mailing every six months. After the comp, wait six months and do a mailing with some clever idea. A couple of Christmases ago, I went home to California for the holidays. About ten days before I came back, I had planned to send out a postcard with a head shot on it. As the winter progressed, I didn't get a head shot and I was getting ready to leave for California. I thought, Well, maybe my high school graduation picture or something. Then I thought, No, wait a minute. I got out my scrapbook, found a picture when I was God only knows how old—five, six?—and designed the card. I mailed it to my client list on the Monday of the week I was coming home. I got back at three o'clock on Wednesday afternoon and from this mailing I had five hundred dollars' worth of booking for Thursday and Friday."

*(Opposite) Forrest's mailers. Today's cowboy: David Robinson.
(Above) Ted Dawson depicts Duke of Windsor, Fred Astaire, Gary
Cooper and James Dean for GQ anniversary issue. Photos: Barry
McKinley. Also, Dawson celebrating his third birthday with
his parents in Malaya.*

Since editorial work is generally more innovative, it helps the established model keep ahead of the advertising market, which eventually follows the lead of editorial. "Editorial is how we establish ourselves," says Kalani Durdan. "It helps get us going. Because of editorial, clients see us and want to use us. Editorial is also the way we refurbish our images."

"Often I kind of rediscover a model," muses Bruce Weber, sometimes called "star-maker" because he has discovered or launched many male models. "By rediscover, I mean maybe it's a model I used three or four years ago. Maybe he's been doing lots of work, yet I haven't used him again. All of a sudden a commercial job will come along and I'll know that guy is right for it. I'll be just as excited as I was the first time I used him. Right now, for a lot of editorial work, I prefer working with guys who haven't modeled all that much. They bring a lot of enthusiasm to the pictures, a kind of raw energy. But for many commercial jobs you really have to have a model with a couple years of experience to be really able to pull it off. Sometimes you have to do maybe ten or twelve pictures a day. The clients are there putting on the pressure. You can't do that with someone who hasn't worked in front of a camera before."

Weber offers an unusual suggestion to models for keeping their careers on target. He thinks models need periodic emotional alterations more than physical changes. "I always think it's good for models to have another job or to get away from the business for a little while, maybe every couple months. They should go out and really deal with people outside the business. It's much healthier than only seeing photographers, art directors and other models and never playing baseball or going sailing. That's where jadedness comes in, and it shows in the photographs, because the models don't have any other life to pull from for the camera. When you're photographing, it's hard to catch something about a model or his life if all he's been doing is modeling.

"The word 'model' is a weird one," he continues. "When you're photographing someone, the last thing in the world you want him to do is *model*. That's the death of the picture."

Weber feels that by trying to expand their clientele, many models lose their essential character or unique quality. "The pity is that so many models forget about themselves and who they are, really. They forget that in the beginning, people wanted to photograph them because they were special, not because they knew how to put on a three-piece suit. The problem stems from the clients, who only want very safe-looking guys. Clients don't want to use models that you think about, particularly any dirty thoughts. They want the type of guy you could take to a party and who'd never offend anybody, who's so bland you forget about him. There is a great pressure for models to look acceptable. A model who looks like the only person in the world is constantly being hit over the head to become just like everybody else. Finally he gives in. Then he looks like your next-door neighbor and doesn't look like the only person in the world anymore. That's where I think a lot of models lose it. I know of one guy I thought was astonishing. He used to be one of my most favorite people to photograph. He had a big broken nose, the most extraordinary nose I'd ever seen. Blue eyes, freckles. He looked like a prizefighter. He looked like nobody else I'd ever seen. His face took light beautifully. Everybody said, 'He's so ugly that he's great-looking,' or 'He looks so weird, so different.' Finally he gave in and really wanted to look like everybody else. He had his nose done, and he got his wish.

"What bothers me the most," Weber continues, controlling his agitation, "is something that trails through a lot of jobs. It's partially the fault of the model and partially the hang-ups of other people in this business, who think that a guy who's modeling is really like a low kind of thing. I wish more models could feel proud about what they're doing. I was photographing for an Italian men's magazine in New York City. I was using a guy who's a fabulous athlete and very, very handsome. The editor from Italy said, 'I think he's poor-looking.' What? 'I don't think he looks strong enough, macho enough, rich enough.' If a man has his own sort of personal dignity and pride, he's going to look like the richest person in the world. He's not going to look like everybody's version of what they think a screaming fag model looks like.

"When you're working and you're constantly hearing comments like that—'He looks poor' or 'I think that guy looks too handsome' or 'That guy looks like he's coming on too much'—you get a little crazy. Why shouldn't that guy look too handsome? Why shouldn't that guy look like he's coming on? And what's wrong with photographing a guy who really is gay looking? Why try to hide it? That's part of him, you know?" By now Weber is pacing.

"People have difficulty in accepting sensuality in men," he goes on. "I think they're really frightened by it. One of my favorite places to work is the *Soho News*, because there you can use any kind of guy you want. You can approach photographing men in any way, shape or form. We did a series of what men wear when the landlord finally turns on the heat in the winter, after all those days when there hasn't been any. It's so hot in your apartment all of a sudden you can't believe it. It was really an underwear and a bathrobe story.

"The reactions we got from those pictures were just *hostile*," says Weber, his eyes wide in disbelief. "A lot of people said, 'Those pictures are pornographic.' Pornographic? We had sat down and thought about it and said, 'How wonderful it would be after years of seeing girls in underwear in *Cosmopolitan*, in *Vogue*, in whatever, to show a guy in underwear and to make the pictures not, 'Oh, there's that guy, he's so plastic,' but more like, 'It wouldn't be so bad to know this guy.' We wanted to show him the same way photographers have shown girls for years." (The *we* Weber mentions are the people he calls "my team"— stylists Kezia Keeble and Paul Cavacco, and hairstylist Bob Fink.) "We got very excited about doing those pictures. How can you say that a

*Reaction to these shots of
Jeff Aquilon in the* Soho
News *stung the photographer.
Photos: Bruce Weber*

picture of a man who is very handsome, lying in a bed that is totally torn apart—you can see the mattress ticking—looking as if he's just made love with somebody or like he couldn't sleep all night, so his feet are all wrapped up in the covers—how can you call that pornographic? What's pornographic about photographing a man in a very private moment? He's lying there in his underwear all curled up. That's the way we all sleep. I think what's pornographic is to put a guy in a jump suit and lay him on a boat with a girl who looks like someone in drag drinking a glass of champagne. To me, that's pornographic.

"It's funny. Something very interesting happened down at the *Soho News* when those pictures came out. We were all just standing around and the publisher came in to say that Saks Fifth Avenue had canceled their advertising for the following week because of those photographs. Everybody applauded and the publisher said, 'Well, I guess we're doing something right.'

"The fact is, here is a person who trusted us to photograph him. For a guy to really open himself up in a picture is a very, very difficult thing to do," says Weber softly, still flushed by the sting of criticism.

But established models often find themselves in a bind. The most consistent source of their income is catalog work, which allows the least room for personal or artistic expression. To discount that work on creative grounds might be personally satisfying but financially devastating. Some models take more rigid personal stands than others.

"Let's say you're having a slow week and a particular low-grade client arrives on your chart," theorizes Denis La Marsh. "It doesn't make sense to do that job just for the sake of filling in a week. That will hurt you in the long run because your better clients will see you doing lesser work. There is always pressure from your agent to take every job that comes along, because your agent wants to make the bread, wants to see you working all the time. You get flak if you turn down jobs, but a model has to keep the reins."

"Now I will only model products that I believe in," says Conrad Bell. "As a designer myself, it would be hypocritical to be seen wearing double knits. So I won't. I won't do shitty catalog work anymore."

Most models will and do. They don't consider what they wear professionally as personal endorsements. Rather, they view their work at this juncture in more philosophical terms. Ed Fry puts it well: "Essentially, the sole reason for a model's existence is to act as a merchandising tool. You are there to sell something, whether it's an article of clothing or a feeling. You are not there because you are lovely or because of your personal vanity. You are there only because you are selling something for someone. That is the only reason the client is paying you."

Rather than seeking new forms of expression, numerous models rely on past performances to insure their future; hence the repetitiveness and the mechanical quality that pervades their working days. They may *want* to be more creative, but they're generally stopped fast. Some bookings are exciting. Most are not. Even when they try to fight it, routine sets in.

So does a reluctance to tell their truthful age, at least among sizable numbers of models. A very successful one—R.D., to make up initials— didn't begin his modeling career until he was thirty-five. "I don't really care about my age," he claims, "but I just question the wisdom of telling people. If you tell someone you're thiry-eight or thirty-nine, even though you look maybe in your early thirties, that person thinks of you in the older category. Someone may not know me, but may read or hear about my age. If a photographer says, 'How about R.D.?' the client will say, 'Oh, R.D. is too old.' It's that kind of thing. Let's just say I started a little later than most people do."

Age isn't the only pitfall. Since models' attitudes necessarily change over the years, sometimes they head off in the wrong direction.

"It seems the more successful models get, the more complaints come in," says Tom Hahn. "In the star category, about fifty percent of the time you get star trips. The guys suddenly feel that things should be easier for them. It's never any easier. You remember a guy who used to be terrific, who used to love to go out and do a job. Suddenly he demands that the catalog studio book him at a minimum of two hours at a hundred dollars an hour. And the studio says, 'Gee, we've only got enough work for an hour.' The model will turn around and say, 'Well, if they want me bad enough, they'll pay the two hours.' He doesn't realize that a smart businessman makes exceptions in those areas. Those people made him who he is. With all the guys coming into this industry, there's more of a chance of getting knocked off the ladder. The more demanding you get, the more times a photographer is going to say, 'Screw him, I don't want to use him.' If you knock off three or four photographers, you cut out a lot of work. You're going to miss a lot of nice work you might have had if you hadn't been such an asshole."

"The worst that can happen is when a model believes his own publicity," suggests Dan Deely. "Models are constantly being told how good-looking they are, how wonderful and fabulous they are. Clients tell this to models while they're working to be supportive. Which is all well and good. Because models are supposed to be great and wonderful and all that. But the minute a model starts thinking that what he's hearing is true—*I am the best*—that's going to come across in his work and in his dealings with people. A model can go downhill just as quickly as he got to the top. Quicker. There's never a job that only one model can fill. If a client has a choice of two models with equally good looks, the model who's the easier to work with is the model who's going to win out. It's natural for the head to swell. Somebody will come out of a zero background working in a drugstore for a dollar twenty-five an hour and all of a sudden is making seven hundred and fifty or a thousand dollars a day. With normal, healthy people, the head swells up. Then somebody kicks you right in the butt and the head comes down again. But a lot of people never come down. They have successful careers for a while and they blow them away."

If not out of civility, the smart model minds his manner out of self-defense.

"Some guys come into the industry and make it very quickly," notes Ken Baker. "The business goes to their heads. They tread on a lot of people, particularly someone they consider lower on the totem pole, maybe the photographer's assistant or the stylist. But today's stylist is tomorrow's booker. Today's assistant is tomorrow's photographer. It does not pay to tread on anybody in this business."

Zoli also thinks it doesn't pay to pick up on a notion that prevails among scores of top models. "The biggest thing to watch out for is to take the business for granted," he says, "to think you've paid your dues. You never pay your dues. When a model thinks, 'I've done it, I'm working very well, I now deserve to live forever and ever making wonderful money,' that's very dangerous. In no profession can you get away with that. You work until you retire. If you don't work at a job, you may get retired against your will. Particularly if you are a male model. Men are much more replaceable. Men don't have the name images. They're still nonentities staring at you from magazine pages. They don't have the publicity like Lauren Hutton or Cheryl Tiegs. They don't get contracts like Lauren Hutton or Cheryl Tiegs. Most girls don't get those contracts either. The law of supply and demand just doesn't work as well for men. There are many more female models, but the demand is far greater for the top girls. A top girl gets booked three to six months in advance, every day. A male model, I would say, two to three weeks. He may have a job or two next June, but still not the demand women enjoy. Clients get upset if a top girl raises her rates, but they'll pay. With a man, they'll often replace him. Girls are the rate setters. Eventually men catch up, then the girls raise their rates again. Men's and women's rates are the same for about a minute. When men's rates rose to a hundred dollars an hour, the top girls raised theirs to a hundred and twenty-five an hour."

Whether men object to the higher rates for women depends upon the nature of the job and the nature of the man. When a man is hired as "atmosphere," usually he doesn't mind the lower fee. However, when the tables are turned (which isn't all that often) and the female is considered the prop, most males feel the woman should not command more than the man. If a man and woman are working as a duo of equals, most male models will raise an outcry for equality.

Another sticky financial subject is the relative lack of discrepancy in rates between beginners and models with years of professional seniority. Michael Edwards voices a fairly typical sentiment when he says, "I don't think it is right for someone who's been working in the business and is really, really good to make a certain rate, and then for someone who's just starting out to make the exact amount of money on a booking. You

Veteran Michael Edwards ponders if beginning models deserve "this incredible money."
Photo: Barry McKinley

are on the job with someone new. You have to help the new person loosen up—which you never mention—and very seldom does anyone on the job see that you are pulling the whole show. I don't think just because someone has a super look that the person should automatically be entitled to get all this incredible money."

Although it's recognized as a sore point, no one is certain how to soothe the situation. "From a selfish outlook, I would say, no, it's not quite fair that someone entering the business should earn as much as someone who's been knocking his head against the wall for years," says Charles Williamson. "Then again, if the rates weren't fairly uniform, more advantage would be taken of models. Truthfully, what matters is the end result. If an ad with a model who's only modeled for three weeks is as successful or even more successful than an ad with somebody who's modeled for ten years, all the more power to the guy who's been at it for three weeks. When seniority takes precedence, that limits quality. Now, the person who has established himself has to keep on his toes and stay ahead. A lot of people have the tendency to get somewhere and, because they have attained this or that, they get on a high horse, so their quality of work isn't nearly as high as when they were trying to make it."

"We are salesmen without any control over our own product," analyzes Scott MacKenzie. "We relinquish all our rights to our agents. Sure, they are out wheeling and dealing for us. But I would like to see the male model have some initiative of his own. I wish stores had contracts that we could negotiate without an agent. Then a model could establish some credibility as a power source and could set up his career according to his own needs. Agents are flesh peddlers and you're the meat."

With many central business issues unresolved, more models are beginning to agree with Brad Bauer's assessment of what the profession needs: "I will sum it up in two words—model union. Unfortunately, the bigger agencies are suppressing the idea because they know if that ever came about, models would have more say-so about rates and commissions."

Bill Carrico has been active in the formation of the Professional Models Association, an idea whose time has not yet come. He admits, "PMA is in limbo right now because we want to have it national and nothing else. We have drawn up a very good contract that has been supported by practically every model in Chicago. The major goal is standardization of policy regarding all the agents and models. That just makes sense. Plus health and welfare benefits, retirement benefits, hospitalization. Even voice artists have a union. It just seems a natural step to have the modeling business set up that way. But we have to have the full support of a large organization to make PMA work. A union has to have power. It won't work on a local level. Starting a models' union has been tried before in other cities and none of them even got as far as we did here. Truthfully, I think the chances of getting PMA going are about ten to one right now. But it'll come. The idea of PMA isn't for the heavyweights, but for the new people, especially the women, who are abused and taken advantage of. I've treated this business as a profession, and as a professional, and I would like to see it on that level at all times. I would like to be proud of what I'm involved in. This business is ninety-eight percent pleasant. I guess I'm looking for that extra two percent."

Certain practices are fairly standard. When it comes to the big-money campaigns—such as cigarette or liquor ads—the advertising agencies establish pay schedules. One model advertising a particular brand of cigarettes earned approximately six thousand dollars in the course of a year from one picture that appeared on billboards and in magazines. However, the specifics in any deal vary, depending on whether transit posters, television, national magazine ads, newspapers and billboards are all involved or if only one or two of these elements come into play.

Although most models prize major campaigns, there is an ongoing worry about what may or may not be a hazard, overexposure. If a model

Bill Carrico: "I guess I'm looking for that extra two percent." Photo: Paul Gremmler

is seen too often, will his career burn out? Loíc Raout, whose favorite national ad is the one he did for Winston Lights, says, "I've been overexposed every year. And my income has been higher every year, so I don't think it's a problem."

"Any temporary work that pays by the hour is extremely unpredictable," remarks Zoli. "There's no formula for what overexposure is. Say a successful model has been working very steadily for the last two or three years. He has at least a page in every catalog, an ad for every department store, is in every magazine constantly, month in, week in, day in, day out. And then he'll do a campaign that is on every bus, in every drugstore window, in every newspaper, and maybe he's also involved in a television campaign. A lot of his clients may say, 'Let's try somebody else.' The minute that happens, that's overexposure. The chances are—hopefully for the established model—that the new model doesn't work out and the client will say, 'That was a mistake. Let's go back to old tried and true.'

"A model who does lots of national ads, national billboards, national everythings, he will be much more quickly overexposed," continues Zoli, "than will a person who is quietly working every day for the catalogs and doing work we don't see every day in New York or L.A. But this overexposure is a funny thing. It doesn't last forever. It may stall a career for a short time. But there is nothing older than last month's magazine. Six months from now, we don't really remember who was in what magazine. So a model's career will pick up again."

Naturally, what models fear most during slow periods is that their career won't pick up again. And sometimes they don't. Sometimes there is no dramatic drop-off, just a deadly gradual decline. A modeling career can drift away before the man's eyes and he may never know why. If he has the stamina, maybe he can regain his courage and his position. Maybe not. After he's been breezing along, a sudden stillness usually precedes an emotional storm.

"It sounds like poor soap opera material," relates a former model, currently working for a small advertising agency outside New York City. He will share his experiences, but not his name. "I lost all belief in myself when my bookings fell off. I literally felt worthless. Maybe I hadn't prepared myself for the fall from grace. I'm not sure. Because I'm not sure why it happened. It isn't like I woke up one morning and my looks had all gone down the drain. I hadn't gained forty pounds or suddenly grown horns. I don't think I had acted like a bastard. I mean, there were still jobs, but I couldn't pay the rent any longer. If I ever thought anything like that would happen—which I don't think I really did—I guess I thought it would happen at forty-five or fifty, not thirty-seven. But, you see, I don't think it had anything to do with age either. I don't think it had anything to do with anything. I know that sounds like bullshit but, honest to God, I can't figure it out. Anyway, get ready to play the violin. I felt unloved. Worse, unlovable. I didn't swallow the sleeping pills, but I stared at them on my night stand every night for a month. The one or two bookings I got, I refused. I didn't leave my apartment. Oh, shit. Look, it was a knife in the bowels. What can I tell you? I'd love to say, 'But I grew as an individual,' or some crock like that. I can't say that. I can't say anything or explain anything. It happened. I thought my whole life was over. It wasn't. Maybe I wasn't smart enough. Maybe I wasn't good enough. Maybe, maybe, maybe. Of course I knew the carousel would stop. But so fast? Am I happy now? Sure, I'm happy. As happy as I was then? I can't say. I'm different now. Not more mature, more cynical, more worldly wise, none of those lies. I had it. I don't have it anymore. I'm older. Not better or worse. What's that line? I don't just remember the good times or the bad times, but the whole damn thing."

No man can speak for *all* men, and no model can speak for all models. Craig Vandenburgh does not. But he has a valiancy in his humor and a grittiness in his outlook that make his comments worth inspection. He cuts through a lot of sham to bare his own truths.

"The way a lot of models talk about modeling drives me up the fucking wall," says Vandenburgh, groaning and laughing at the same time. "You watch Merv Griffin or David Susskind. They'll have models on those talk shows to discuss the field of male modeling. (I don't know why they call it male modeling. You can only be a female or a male model. Unless you are up for sexual reassignment.) Now, the night before they have those shows about modeling, Merv Griffin or David Susskind will do a program about women with mastectomies or men dying

(Opposite) "I've been overexposed every year,"
says Loíc Raout. Photo: Barry McKinley

of terminal cancer of the testicles. Those are heavy topics. The next night, they'll have something light, like modeling. But the people who have mastectomies talked more lightly about themselves than the models do. 'It is really tough, there is nothing glamorous about it, we're not treated like human beings, I can't stand it, I hope I can get out of modeling soon.' Well, it is very easy. Just refuse ever to work again and get yourself a job at Woolworth's. What the fuck would those people do if they weren't modeling? I always go crazy whenever I hear anyone talking about modeling. I think eighty percent of us are egomaniacs. Correct that. Ninety percent.

"We love being looked at. We love being the center of attention. There's nothing wrong with that. I would much rather be standing on a stage with people screaming at me than be backstage pulling the curtain. I would much rather be in the center of a room being photographed in a pair of pants than be on my knees pinning the pants. Modeling just for the money is one of the biggest lies ever started. There are too many other ways in the world to make money for somebody to turn to modeling to make money.

"I never thought I'd be a model. I've always felt very homely—very, very ugly. I am not just saying that to be cute or clever. I really have. I went to a psychiatrist in college because I thought I was so ugly I might have to have plastic surgery or else wear a surgical mask. That is how bad I was. He thought I was crazy. He said, 'You're not going to sit there and tell me you're ugly.' I said, 'I'm not paying you to tell me I'm good-looking. I look like hell.'

"I left school and the shrink and became an actor. I always played character parts. I would never ever do a romantic lead because who would fall in love with me? I remember trying to sing when I was younger. I couldn't sing love songs because I couldn't imagine someone ever being in love with someone who looked like me.

"I came back from summer stock. I needed new pictures. A friend, a model, sent me to a photographer. I said I only wanted funny head shots. He suggested we do one serious one and I said it would be of no use to me. When he saw the contacts, he called and said, 'You should be a model.' I said, 'You're crazy.'

"But I was working as a movie usher and making forty dollars a week. So I went to an agent. I was sent on a go-see, got the job and was off to England. I was the first model who had hair over his ears. Before then, a model had to cut his hair every two weeks and be very, very neat. I came back and started working like crazy right off the bat. It was not at all difficult. I was thrilled that I was able to make so much money so easily. Plus, it was like being a movie star. Wanting to be an actor, all that attention was fabulous. I was the HIS symbol. I had endless ads and editorials. Just unbelievable. Everybody knew me and it was a marvelous feeling. There is so little to learn compared to other businesses or professions it's hardly worth talking about. You sit down, you stand up, you

walk to the left, you walk to the right, you smile. A lot of models feel very guilty about making so much money. There is no reason to feel guilty about it. But obviously they do because they go on and on about how difficult modeling is. Bullshit. I love it when they say things like, 'In the winter, you have to wear bathing suits and you're freezing. In the summer, you're wearing sweaters.' Well, go to the garment district and see the guys pushing racks of dresses through the streets in the summertime. Would you rather be doing that in the summer than wearing a sweater for a hundred dollars an hour? I bet the guy pushing the rack of dresses would sure as hell change places with you. Tell me about the strain of doing catalog work. How does a ballet dancer feel at the end of the show? How does a singer feel after two hours in concert? They don't get on TV and say how tired they get or complain about getting a sore throat. If a model isn't happy now, stick around twenty years, baby, and then let the real hell break loose. There is so much puritanical crap in all of us. We have to make modeling into an ordeal because joy and pleasure are not allowed. Why not, for Christ's sake? All these models are so fucking guilty. It's difficult to get up in the morning and put on clothes and go ride horses at some multimillionaire's home in Virginia and get paid a thousand dollars? If you have to go to a factory and glue pins together to pay the rent, it's not so fucking difficult.

"Modeling is extremely glamorous. I can't think of anything more glamorous. It's more glamorous than show business. If you do a one-man show like I'm doing now, you are doing the same thing over and over and over. Doing comedy, doing anything in show business, is a great deal of work and a great deal of monotony. And it is very lonely. People are out there every night, but you don't meet that many people.

"Modeling is also glamorous because you are strictly being paid because you are some kind of object of beauty. Man has admired beauty from the beginning of time. As a model, you possess this beauty that cannot be bought. It cannot be created. You can write every book in the world about looking good, dressing right, fucking yourself up. Those books can't make any difference. Either you look like shit or you look great, and there ain't much you can do.

"A model is someone who rents out his body by the hour to be looked at or to be photographed. Period. It is renting out what you are physically endowed with. For a price. There is nothing wrong with that. It feels good and it's fun. But most models try to make it into some great creative thing. Or something they hate doing. Or something they never wanted. And yet they never willingly leave it. It's like people who complain about being rich. 'Oh, it's so boring being rich, darling.' If money is such a problem, throw it away. Give it to charity. Come and live in my dump on Fifteenth Street. If you think modeling is difficult, leave the agency. Find the real world. *I* have been trying to avoid it all my life.

"In the beginning, I was very unusual-looking to people. I had a very offbeat look. I wasn't All-American looking at all. There were no European models with my agency when I started. I went to England. I came back. And I was known for a very specific look. The English Mod look, or whatever it was called. Wild pants and wild shirts. The Rolling Stones were big, the Beatles were big. I was specifically identified with a certain look, a certain type of person, a certain *period*. Elvis Presley went out of fashion when the Beatles came in. In its tiny way, it was the same thing with me.

"I was at the top for two years. Working all the time. And then the Mod look was over and no one knew what to do with me. I was known for one thing and it passed.

"It was very upsetting and difficult. But, except for those two years when I was really a big model, my whole life has been very difficult and very changeable. Moving every year when I was a kid, I never really fit in with people. I was used to living with crises. In fact, when things are good, I become almost terrified.

"Modeling was a marvelous surrogate for stardom for a while. Every dog has his day and mine is definitely gone. So now I've got to get out there and try to become a star making people laugh. I'm working on a new act now. Pure comedy. *The Village Voice* came to review me and wrote, 'Show biz to the core.' The *Daily News* said, 'Promising new male counterpart to Lily Tomlin's brand of characters in the world.' But it is much, much harder. Because modeling is so fucking easy, it spoils you for almost anything else in life.

"When those two years were over, it was upsetting. I wouldn't say devastating. But I couldn't give up modeling entirely. I kept trying to do it because I liked it so much and it was such an easy way to live. It was so scary to have to get a regular job. And I'd be in these awful little

Craig Vandenburgh
A recent portrait
Photo: Ken Haak

Broadway shows. It was hard going from working with top photographers and top people as a top model to working with shlumps in show biz, going from beautiful dressing rooms to some dirty rehearsal hall on Avenue A.

"Modeling never really became that good again. I was able to make a living off it, but not a fantastic living. With many lean years. But it is just something I've done for so long now, I can't imagine not doing it.

"The only thing I would change about modeling is the age factor. If I had my way, there would be models who are a hundred. Modeling is such a pleasurable field to me. I would do anything if I could just freeze the way I looked five years ago and somehow never go out of style. For a long time, I thought my agency would drop me. I thought I'd just be told, 'We don't need you anymore.' Now, I don't think that's going to happen for a while, because it would be pretty damn hard to replace me. There are very few calls for me, but where are they going to get new models in my age range? There aren't that many guys at thirty-five deciding, 'I think I'll give up my bank and go model.'

"I think for many of us, it is never, ever going to be as good as it was when we were big models. We can think it will be and that we are going to become this and we are going to become that. I think for most of us, it will never be as good."

A light moment on the set. While the hairdresser works, Lynn Coleman plays with Tony Spinelli. Photo: Barry McKinley

CHAPTER 6

basic black

July 30, 1967, was a hot, clear day in Manhattan. That morning a young computer programmer trainee, skipping a day of work, took the bus from Newark into the city. As he walked along Seventh Avenue, his hair in the pronounced Afro style of the time, he felt (as he now describes the sensation) that the umbilical cord connecting his life to New Jersey was severed. Word was out that designer Bill Blass was looking for black male models for an upcoming fashion show. Dressed in khaki pants and a striped button-down shirt, without portfolio and without experience, he entered the imposing Blass reception area.

Several minutes later he was back on Seventh Avenue, the gist of the short interview, "Don't call us, we'll call you." He noticed a phone booth. He flipped through the Yellow Pages and located listings for modeling agencies. Ford was the only name that registered. Short on pocket change, he walked to the East Fifty-ninth Street address and mounted the steep stairs.

"You are too tall, you have a scar on your nose, and there is no demand for black men. Thank you," were the words of discouragement. He hesitated. "Listen, don't take our word," he was told. "A new agency has just opened up. It's called Wilhelmina. Why don't you go over there and see what they have to say?"

Lunching at a coffee shop, glancing at his reflection in the mirrored wall, he made a decision. Acting the innocent was getting him nowhere. Perspiration beaded on his forehead when he asked the receptionist at Wilhelmina to show him the agency's headsheet.

"You only have one black man," he pointed out. "And he doesn't even look black. Look at that hair. I am very disappointed. I'm from the NAACP, and I'm looking into what efforts are being made by modeling agencies to help the cause. I would like to speak to someone in authority here."

Today, Renauld White, credited as the first black male model to climb to the top echelon of the profession, is sheepish discussing his impersonation.

"I wouldn't want people to get the wrong idea," he says. "But I was pissed. Black men should look like black men. I got irate, and the actor in me took over. The receptionist was all bothered. I was shown into an office, and then I knew I had it made. I was introduced to a woman, the bookkeeper. I didn't know then that she was a part owner in the agency. I repeated my story, adding that I wanted to model, and that if I didn't hear any good reason why I could not, I'd have pickets outside their agency the next morning. Other agency people got into the act, saying they didn't want any trouble but that no one was going to tell them what models to represent. Now, this discussion went on and on for more than an hour. I just stood my ground. Inside, I was shaking. I was a *kid*. But I felt something had to be done, I really did. Finally, the woman said to me, 'Well, how do we know if you are salable or not? Because we can't tell. Look at your hair, it's out to here. Look at your sideburns, they're down to there. We can't tell what your face looks like because we can't see it.' I said, 'Fine, if that's all you want, I'll come back. I'll get my hair cut and I'll be back tomorrow.' So I borrowed some money from a friend, got my hair cut off, cut my sideburns, bought a new pair of pants, borrowed a shirt, and went back. I was told, 'There is a *possibility*. Here is your contract.' Now, this is something you only see in movies. I don't think you ever hear of anybody really bullshitting his way into modeling."

Whatever his tactics, his belief in himself has been vindicated. If White had not acted out the charade, the market for black models would likely be even narrower than it is today. White was not in the right place at the right time: he created a place when the time was not ripe.

"I think they thought giving me the contract would be the end of it," the model recalls, "that all I really wanted was to dangle this prized possession—that contract—in front of people. They assumed I'd get discouraged and that would be that. Little did they know. If you give me one inch, I'm going to take it to the maximum." White stayed with Wilhelmina for four years before shifting to Zoli Men.

"When I was growing up, I had no one to look at in magazines," he continues. "I fantasized like everybody else. Going to the movies on Saturdays and looking at Marlon Brando and James Dean or whomever. But I never had a black man to look at and say, 'Hey, he is terrific, I would like to emulate him.' It wasn't there. At that point, there were a few black men modeling, but you never saw a black man doing any editorial. You never saw a black man advertising products that weren't specifically for blacks."

Renauld White
Photo: John Ford

But you were told to change your hair and sideburns. Did you feel that you were being molded into the white man's version of an acceptable black male?

"I didn't feel that right away. I was so excited about getting one foot in the door that I probably welcomed change. I wanted it so bad that I could not see anything other than success. I felt that this was such a far-out shot, how it happened to me, that I would go along with this one demand. And cutting my hair was not too unreasonable."

What was your family's reaction?

"My family thought it was ridiculous, my giving up a perfectly good Establishment job. They'd hoped I'd be a computer operator."

Were they disappointed?

"I don't think so. My family expressed a lot of enthusiasm for whatever I wanted to do."

But they had some reservations?

"Some. Because they knew it was going to be very difficult for me, that I was going to be hurt. They realized there was a rough struggle ahead. Because it had never been done before. And here I was all excited. I think they believed in me but they realized it was not going to happen the way I thought it was going to happen. Some thought I'd go back to the life that I knew, working in an office. No. No. I never once thought I was going back to that kind of life. I had a taste of modeling and I wanted it bad."

Was there something specific you wanted from modeling?

"Not really. Although I did fantasize about being the first black man on the cover of *GQ*."

In fact, you were not. A black man didn't make that cover until November 1977. He was a young European model.

"I never bought that issue."

Did that really hurt?

"Yes, it hurt. Because twice before that I thought I was going to be on the cover, and both times got shot down. I wish the first had been an American black man. It was pretty painful."

Back to the beginning. Did you encounter racism?

"Once I did a shooting for *Esquire*, which I thought was a real breakthrough, but when the pictures appeared, they were all cropped at my chin. You never saw my face. The fashion editor called to apologize, said he had nothing to do with that."

Did you have difficulties testing?

"I did. I really did. First of all, models aren't born. I firmly believe that most models are not born. They are groomed. I had to find my own style, my *own*. I had to find my own center. I had to deal with New York City, which is contemporary Babylon. I had to pull it together and break through the cold advertising world. I knew from nothing. I found that I had to go above and beyond. There I was, an odd man in an even world.

It was just difficult to adjust to. I was working nights as a waiter, traveling back and forth to Newark."

What were the go-sees like?

"I couldn't think of them just as go-sees. I had to go and convince clients that I was the man they wanted to use. I had to inspire them to use me. I went around with the intention of putting something into the art director's mind. I had a work plan. First, I had to make myself known, so that later maybe someone would say, 'Hey, let's work with him.' One of my first bookings was advertising Vitalis, which is basically a white Establishment product. The client thought I would be good to grab the black market. And it worked. As a result, I was written up in *Advertising Age*. There were three men in the ad, two white men and myself. It got a lot of attention. I think it sort of brought the light to a lot of clients that black people existed as a market for white products, or, rather, that products aren't exclusively racial."

When you were a guest on the Phil Donahue Show, *he said you have "the world's most beautiful scar right on your nose." How did you get that scar?*

"Well, it wasn't plastic surgery. I got hit with a baseball bat when I was six years old. I was running around being frivolous. My aunt was playing baseball, showing off in front of the boys. She was up at bat and was a little overweight at the time—a *lot* overweight. I ran up behind her just as she was swinging and *Pow!* I caught it. I was splattered. Thank God, it has certainly worked for me. At the time, it made me a very unattractive child who used to sit on his steps with a handkerchief over his face. Kids can be very cruel."

Did you have reconstructive surgery?

"No. The fortunate thing is that my uncle was a doctor. His office was on the first floor of the house where I lived. And being a quack doctor"—White winks—"he left a scar. I thank him to this day."

Initially did the scar present problems?

"Not too many. If clients didn't want it, they would just airbrush it out. And I would say to myself, 'That's not me, that perfect nose.' Sometimes clients would ask if I'd cover it up with makeup. But they've stopped doing that. They know me. The scar is my trademark. I don't mind being a scar-faced man."

A woman in the Donahue audience asked how the females you date feel when you are prettier than they. Remember your answer?

"Not exactly."

"I date a couple of models, so it's even." The audience loved that remark. But has your sex life changed as a result of modeling?

"Has my sex life changed? They named a holiday after my sex life. It's called Passover."

True?

"Let's set the record straight. If I lived up to the reputation that people think models have—Warren Beatty used the line once, I think—I'd be in a jar in the Smithsonian. If models did everything we're supposed to be doing how could we ever get up to make our bookings?"

Have you become more selective?

"I have always selected. I have never settled."

Do you receive fan mail?

"Yes, I do. A lot. I think it's wonderful. Mostly from young girls. Some young girls and young men interested in modeling. But primarily from young girls who have fantasized about me and who have seen me over the years. They send me pictures, and they say I remind them of a cousin. I always look like someone's cousin. I got an incredible amount of mail from all over the United States from being on the *Phil Donahue Show*. I tried to answer most of them, which is not easy because I don't have a secretary. I have faithful fans out there who write me notes and send me Christmas cards. I love it. I hope it never stops."

Do you ever get off-the-wall letters?

"No. But I'm waiting."

Have you ever walked off a set?

"Ah, yes. Yes, I have."

Under what circumstances?

"Well, it was not a set. I was given an outfit to wear. I refused. It made me look like one of those lantern statues in the yard. I just felt that today no black man should be seen in that outfit."

What are the opportunities for black models today compared to the later sixties and early seventies?

"There is the same amount of work but there are more black models. The work for black women has increased, but black men are still the lowest on the totem pole. It hasn't really opened up for us. I don't know what can be done about it. Maybe it's the government choosing priorities other than advertising, such as welfare and hospitalization, rather than trying to get more black people on the pages of magazines and newspapers. But I think it is very important for black people to have good images to look at, to emulate. If I go back home, when I walk down the street and see some kids and they say, 'Hey, man, love what you're doing,' that says it all, that's *it*. Now that I'm doing it, these kids can say, 'Hey, I know him. He's from my home town.' "

What do you think of modeling schools?

"I don't believe in modeling schools at all. Perhaps for women. Schools might give them some sort of self-confidence. As far as a man goes, you can't teach him anything in a modeling school. It's all on-the-job training. The reality is in the doing. Schools can't guarantee you anything. They're only good at taking your money."

Certain schools deliberately try to entice black men.

"If I meet a guy on the street who expresses a desire to model but I know does not meet the qualifications, I won't try to discourage him.

I will never be negative to another black person. But I'll always say, 'Find out firsthand. Look in the Yellow Pages. Let the top agencies in New York explain the requirements. If you meet the qualifications, then you're in. If you don't, forget it.' "

Have you ever thought that, instead of representing a role model, you may represent an impossible dream?

"I represent hard work, self-discipline and a desire to better my life. I totally feel that you can break out of your environment if you so desire. I didn't have what it took in the beginning. It was a rude awakening for me. But I was mature enough to realize I had to work at a goal. If I had been five feet nine inches tall, I would have realized I was being unrealistic about modeling. People are smart enough to know they can't pay bucks for the impossible. Perhaps someone can't model, but maybe he could be an actor. If someone feels within his soul he was not meant to be just another mediocre person, then by God he'll find a way to work at being the best of whatever he sets out to be."

But aren't a number of young black men seizing upon modeling as a potential career because they can't see another way out?

"Yes, that happens. But you must realize that black men have always been very closely associated with fashion. They love to sport their finery. It has given them incentive to model even though they don't meet the requirements. Not every white guy who wants to model meets the requirements, does he? The *desire* isn't what's wrong. What's wrong is to manipulate that desire for selfish reasons. Within the black environment, there are always people dangling promises. There are always charlatans saying, 'If you pay me this, I'll promise you that.' That is the American way. And we all know that the American way is not always the right way. But there is nothing I can do about that. I wish I could, but I can't. I can only repeat: Go right to the most important source. If you haven't got it, then channel your energy somewhere else, for God's sake. Don't throw away your hard-earned money. But, more important, don't get discouraged either. Because we all have a lot of valuable things to give. What we as black men need is more brotherhood with each other. We haven't really been able to put our arms around each other and to say, 'Hey, I believe in you, I am proud of you.' Because that hasn't been happening lately. We need that. *I* will never discourage anyone who comes up to me and says he wants to model even if he's five feet five inches tall. How can I do that? Who am I? I'm not going to bust anyone's dreams. I am not."

But their dreams will get busted anyway.

"Yes. But not by me." White shakes his head and smiles grimly. "So maybe they'll pay six hundred dollars for a portfolio that they can show their grandchildren."

The American way. What more do you want from modeling?

"Longevity."

Do you want something outside of modeling?

"I would like very much to move into acting. I've already done a film. I was in *The Stepford Wives*. But I must say, if it doesn't happen, I won't feel as if my life has been incomplete. I don't live for the future and I can't change the past. My whole attitude toward life is not to be safe. I've lived from day to day. So I don't assume anything."

What's the best thing you've gotten from modeling?

"Growing. Just being able to meet people and travel. And being able to work with wonderful people. Not to mention the money. The rewards have been great. I'm one of the few black men in the world making a living in this profession. I have the time and money to just travel alone and have wonderful experiences. Last year I wanted to go to Brazil and I figured, who else could go to Brazil for Christmas and also buy Christmas gifts? Modeling is a wonderful profession. I can't imagine anything else I might have done that could have given me as much joy."

Tempering White's happiness is his ongoing frustration that opportunities for black models are still severely limited. All major agents concede that whereas there is a deluge of black men intent on modeling careers, there is a drought of actual work. The finger of blame is always pointed at advertisers who persistently cast white models in vastly greater numbers than blacks. Agents insist that they cannot take on greater numbers of black models because they would be undermining those models already on their books: if many more black models were represented without a corresponding increase in bookings, they reason that established black models would lose work and that the newer models would still not receive enough bookings to support themselves. How many pieces can the pie be cut into so that every man gets his just dessert? the agents ask. No one says the black male model situation is just; it just *is*.

One rationale offered by advertisers to justify the disproportionately large use of white models compared to racial demographics is that white models can be used to sell products to the mainstream black man, but that the mainstream white man cannot identify with a black man and therefore cannot identify with any product represented by a black model. The admitted exception to this theory is athletes. Supposedly all mainstream men, white or black, can identify with all athletic heroes, black or white; hence the splurge of athletes of both colors endorsing male-oriented products of all kinds. But concerning fashion, one booker for catalogs admits, "The clients always tell us what clothes to put the black person in. In my opinion, I often think they put a black person in an item they don't think is going to sell."

"What the black man is identifying with more than the model is the clothes," believes Charles Williamson, who like nearly all black models resents the paucity of assignments for black men, despite his finally breaking through many barriers himself. "The *GQ* readership is largely

Charles Williamson
Photos: Barry McKinley

a black readership. Yet the ratio of black models doesn't reflect that. There aren't any black publications for a black man to look to where fashion is concerned. So we have to turn to the white magazines. White men aren't going to look at black magazines for fashion because even black men don't want to look at them for fashion. It shouldn't be a matter of black publications versus white publications. It should be: this is *fashion*. The best models should work, whatever their color.

"What modeling for black people basically still is, putting it bluntly, is tokenism," Williamson continues hotly. "Even though there was a fifteen percent increase in 1978 in the men's modeling business, there was no way near that increase in business for black male models as a whole. I would assume that it is more difficult for black models simply because there are more black models coming into the business and the demand is the same. Things are a little more open than they used to be. At least for me. It is my time. It has come. Partly because the market has changed, not a lot, but a bit. Partly because my look has improved. Partly because I'm with a new agency. But, specifically, I believe it has more to do with me. I have been in this business for over seven years. Anyone who has lasted more than seven years and has gone through all the trials and tribulations, people are going to look at.

"Just before I shifted to Elite—that was in December 1977—I was really frustrated with this business. I was really getting sick and tired of all the bullshit and not working. I'd been driving a cab for two years. Twelve hours a night, five nights a week. And I'd get up in the morning and make my rounds. It's very frustrating when you are constantly beat-

ing the pavement and not seeing anything come out of it. It was just my willpower that kept me going. I saw guys come into the business and within a year they were making much more money than I am making now. It had nothing to do with their willpower or what effort they put into it. Some guys just make it. But I had to create my own demand."

Although modeling in general is very competitive, the competition can become more intense among black models, even when they consciously struggle to hold that competitiveness at bay. "It's unrealistic for me to feel that I'm going to get all the work," remarks Williamson, "utterly ridiculous. I don't worry that Renauld is doing this, is doing better than me. Sure, on an emotional level, I tend to feel, Well, look at this person, he's being more accepted than me, and when your emotions get in the way, they can be destructive."

(Renauld White expresses similar sentiments: "Well, there's so little work around that Charles and I are a majority of the time sent out on the same go-sees, even though we don't really look alike. Yes, in a sense we're competing, all black models are competing with each other. Charles and I always speak. I treat him like a gentleman because Charles *is* a gentleman. Still, I try to be my best at all times.")

Commenting on keeping emotions under control, Williamson states, "I believe it's very possible that black models feel an extra strain because we're dealing in a business where there's not that much work. To me, what that really means is that I have to work harder, that's all. We all have to work harder to get the same thing that some other models will get without working as hard. In most any ad, it's the white person who takes precedence. If either model takes precedence, ninety-five percent of the time, it's the white model. On an emotional level, it does not feel very good.

"If you're not careful, your emotions can destroy you," he asserts. "You have to keep the business in its proper perspective. I am not saying I am not in it for my ego. But you've got to be careful of your ego. A lot of people in this business—models, photographers, clients, whomever—treat other people like shit. They forget that they are human beings and they forget that, really, this business is absurd. Advertising is a farce, a lie. How can you have real truth where there is so much phoniness? By any human standards, it is meaningless, actually. But a lot of people, if you took this business away from them, would go crazy. They would jump out the window."

The competitive nature of the profession makes many black models feel that they must outperform not only their black peers but white models as well, regardless what city they work in. San Francisco's Edward Blair says, "The difference between being cast as a black face and being cast as a California blond is this: In the last three years, I've done about fifty commercials. Ninety-five percent of the time I was cast—and it's the same in print—because the clients wanted a black face. The fact that that face belonged to Edward Blair was quite secondary. And

Edward Blair
Photo: Dennis Geaney

you'll hear, usually second-hand, about racial slurs. The client doesn't want a black in a particular picture because the clothing looks too expensive. That doesn't happen to a California blond. The client has to put the black model in the cheap clothing? You die a little bit inside. The only thing you can do is recognize ignorance for what it is. So you do the best job you can. If there's one black and three whites, you do the best job. We have to, black people do, quite frankly. Because ninety-nine percent of the time I've been cast because I have a black face. There has only been that one percent of the time when I've gone into an interview where the caster has looked past the color of a person's nose. You look at the story board for the commercial and you see that the character you're playing was not a black person in the drawing, that the role was open or possibly even meant for a white person. When I get that job, I feel good, knowing I am wanted for my ability.

"That's why I get angry when I hear questions like, 'Is there enough opportunity for black models?'" Blair goes on, his jaw rigid. "Saying 'enough' is putting a ceiling. When does benign neglect take over? Do we benignly neglect the Italian community or the Irish community? Ideally, a model is taken on his worth. We know that's an ideal that this culture is a long way from realizing. I've been knocked on the head in Birmingham. And, quite frankly, I have more important things to do with my life than have an absurd sheriff knock me on the head. Now what I want to do is the best I can."

Eddie Davis
Photo: E. J. Carr

At least one model in Dallas, Eddie Davis, feels work for black men is finally on the upswing. Not that the business climate is perfect there either. "The thing about Dallas is the clients," he remarks. "Some stores will not use black models. I guess they are not ready. But some stores that weren't using blacks when I started are using us today. When I started [approximately three years ago], I would look in the fashion section and I never saw a black. That was one of my goals, to get in there. And I have. Dallas, Texas, has taken a while to realize blacks wear clothes just like everybody, but it is much better than it was.

"A couple years ago, the work just wasn't coming. It got to be a bitch. At first, I knew I had the looks and what it takes, the body and all that, but people wouldn't use me. Then, I started working. Wham, a slow period. I didn't know that's what it actually was, a *slow* period. For everybody. But I couldn't see that. Some of the guys were working, but not that many. I just wanted to give it up. Because I was living in the house, my wife was working and taking care of the bills. I wasn't bringing anything in. I got so depressed, so discouraged. But I got through that period and realized models have slow periods and fast periods. When the season is slow, that's the time to go out and visit clients.

"When I first started out, several people said, 'You'll never make it.' They never said why, they just said it. I was determined to make them all liars. I did and I have. And I've only scratched the surface. I love it." Davis's eyes are laughing, and so is he. "I love the freedom. I love the shows. I love the fittings. I love it all. I love to come down to the agency. I would say to anybody who wants to model, get ready to be torn apart. But it's worth it. To be the best—not the best black model, but the best *model*—that is what I want and that is what I'm going to be."

At the risk of oversimplification, it appears that all top black male models share Davis's resolution to be preeminent. While many of their white counterparts speak disparagingly of the business (perhaps to ward off charges that only the shallow or the star-struck extol it), most black models are extravagant with their praise, except for the large criticism that many doors are effectively shut to members of their race. There's only small consolation in the words of New York agent Zoli: "I have to say, yes, it is harder for a black model to get established. However, once established, the possibility of a black model making more money is excellent. It has happened many times."

It has also happened many times that black men have been forthrightly barred from the profession even though they fit the bill in all ways except one—skin color. If only a few aspiring models ever reach the pinnacle, it's rarer still for a black man to scale the heights. The successes of those who've climbed against the odds to the top should make the journey less torturous for those who would like to follow them. In actuality, though, any indication that male modeling's complexion is ready for a drastic change is probably an optical illusion.

dream lovers

Among my least well-guarded secrets is that I did a nude shooting when I was in my early twenties. I never broadcasted the fact, but things like that have a way of getting known and never forgotten. Some people in the business have seen those pictures and we have chuckled and laughed about them. I pretend blackmail and all that, and it's just kind of fun. I was a kid having an adventure.

Now I know that the consensus is that nude modeling leads nowhere as far as legit modeling is concerned. One does not necessarily lead to the other and, in fact, can harm it. Well, great. I didn't know that at twenty-two, right after I got out of the navy. I was looking for my first apartment and the one I wanted cost more money than I had.

One night I was out having drinks and I was approached by this guy who said he was a photographer and that he'd like to do some pictures of me. I asked, "For what?" He didn't hem or haw, he just said he worked for a company that did mailers of people nude to the Midwest and that people bought these pictures. I said, "I certainly would not be interested, thank you very much," conveying a how-dare-you attitude. He smiled nicely, said, with this little glint in his eye, "Fine. But why don't you take my card in case you change your mind? It's fifty dollars an hour." I took the card.

I went through the whole thing: I have no qualms about nudity; I'm not ashamed of my body; I'm a free person; I'm open; who cares? I needed the money to pay the security for the apartment. Besides, I thought it might be fun.

About a week later I called him. I went over to do this shooting of seminude and nude photographs that were to be mailed to the

Michael Taylor
Body Study
Photo: Ken Haak

Midwest through a small mail-order house. There was to be nothing pornographic about them.

His studio was at his house. I went there and I was nervous. I was dressed in Levis, tennis shoes, who knows. I was so nervous he suggested I have a drink or two. Which I promptly put away. At first we did shots with just the shirt off. Then the ones with the Levi buttons unbuttoned. There was no notion of a strip. There was no notion—just however I felt comfortable, which wasn't very. As I got a little more uninhibited, I thought: What is this about? For Christ's sake, strip and get out of here. I took off all my clothes, he took the pictures, I got my little check right there, and I left. I was delighted. I had a hundred bucks to pay the security for my apartment.

Well, those photographs only showed up in every magazine in every single off-color bookstore in the world. I had friends around the country writing to say, "Glad to see your career is going so well."

They weren't pornographic. I didn't have an erection. In that sense, they were very safe. And also very goofy. I looked like this dazed person drifting around a drafting board. I was bare-ass with a T-square.

To tell the truth, I'm not sorry I did the shooting. I thought I should be sorry, but I wasn't. And I'm not. Except that they weren't the best pictures. If they had been absolutely beautiful pictures, I suppose I would have been delighted to have them out. But they were just insipid.

In '73 or '74, I was doing a shooting with a very legit photographer in the city, a fashion shooting in New York, and he had been commissioned by *Playgirl* to do several covers, several centerfolds, and several new discoveries for X amount of dollars. During that fashion shooting, he asked me if I would be interested. I think that he said it paid $3,000. He also said that after the shooting I could select the pictures I wanted to run and that those would be the only pictures he would send the magazine. I thought, Shit, $3,000 would be fine. He took some Polaroids of me nude and sent them to *Playgirl* for approval. And the response was, Yes, we'd like to use Michael for the centerfold.

We started early in the morning. We went to a secluded beach. I was fishing. With my pants on. Fishing in the ocean. Very active and animated. Then I started to undo my pants. I froze. I thought: What the hell am I doing? I couldn't figure out what I wanted out of the exposure, forgive the pun. I didn't need it for my ego. I guess my ego was satisfied that *Playgirl* wanted me to do the damn thing. That was enough. Period. It was worth $3,000 to me not to do that shooting. I figured I had a career investment in not doing it.

The photographer was fine. We had lunch instead.

I have done nude tests since then. Just as tests. Not for publication. The initial real appeal, I think, is the vicarious thrill that you are appreciated for your physicalness. It's a definite acknowledgment of your desirability in the universe if someone appreciates your physical-ness enough to want to photograph you in your entirety. No clothes, no props. *You.*

Personally, I love to model nude. I find it sensual. I find it sexual. I love it. I think it's a very beautiful, if self-indulgent, form of ex-pression. Unfortunately, you can't do all that much of it and have a legitimate career.

Modeling nude is totally you. What can be more you? I think that almost any male who is not ashamed of his body and who is in the field of modeling somewhere has a desire to model all of him, to have all of him appreciated. That's why a lot of men test in the nude, just for that satisfaction. It's erotic if you are a sensual person. If you're not a sensual person, nothing's erotic.

You know, there is a lot of blather about how nude modeling can ruin a career. I'm sure in many ways that's why I turned down the *Playgirl* thing at the last moment. Just the other day I went on a go-see for a perfume ad that involved nudity. And I went with Zoli's blessing. So there is a certain hypocrisy about this whole question. But did my drifting like a sleepwalker around that drafting table have any detrimental effect on my career? None. Zilch. And I got my apartment.

—*M.T.*

Sex Symbol.

That two-word phrase, like the word "model," carries a female con-notation. If a male model is suspect, a man who poses nude is thought to be a truly suspicious character. A bare ass may be grudgingly ac-ceptable to the public, but hardly ever a bared penis. If the member is flaccid, eyes will probably be averted. If it is even slightly engorged, moral indignation will surely ensue.

Not that female models who frolic nakedly in print are awarded ex-travagant praise. Yet their exposure is not nearly as threatening to society as males exhibiting their genitals. Female models appear naked time and again in *Vogue* without causing a stir, but when male model Pat Anderson bared his bottom in that same magazine, he made the gossip columns. *Playboy* may be a bane of feminism, but *Playgirl* with its masculine centerfolds is viewed the far more objectionable and outrageous of the two by the populace at large, and *Playguy*, which carries male nudism to higher heights, has been called even seamier.

Admittedly, some magazines offering exposed males are more carnal than others. However, outside the realm of pulp and inside the world of art, even when the photographs are taken by imagists with superior credentials—Skrebneski and Ken Haak come to mind—most Americans are discomfited faced with photos of men in the raw.

Central to this double-standard response is our society's difficulty in perceiving the human form, particularly the male body, as beautiful. Nudity is associated with snickers and giggling. An entire feature length film was made for general release a few years back around the one-liner title, *What Do You Say to a Naked Lady?* Yet even the most permissive producer could foresee box office dilemmas with *What Do You Say to a Naked Gentleman?* In a distorted sexist way, it is all right to witness—and snicker or giggle at—female nudity, but not male nudity. Since men are reputedly more prone to sexual arousal via visual stimulation than women, pictorial representations of the female anatomy are supposedly geared to appeal to men, while pictorial representations of the male anatomy are supposedly aimed at homosexual men: male models who show it all are Dream Lovers inciting wet dreams. *If* these photos were perceived as lubricating fantasies of women, not to be seen by other men, they might be less objectionable. This type of thinking artfully begs the question of whether or not nude photography is an art, while also sidestepping the issue of whether or not the human body is a work of art.

Jimmy Grimmé: "I won't take a model if I find out he's done any pornofilms or if he's ever modeled in a gay magazine. I won't touch him. I'm not speaking of fashion layouts. But I will not allow centerfolds. No nudie stuff. Up until a couple years ago, doing centerfolds was not really looked down upon. But so many magazines nowadays are getting homosexual feelings about them. Even your straight magazines. Let's face it, if you're spending a million a year and you're picking a theme boy, you want to make sure that that boy has not appeared in some magazine completely unclothed, lying there like: Take me. It doesn't keep up the image. Let's face it, that's what modeling is. It's an image, a psychological thing. Maybe if I drink milk, I will look like him."

Tom Hahn: "I would never turn down a model who has done nude work as long as it wasn't to the point of being pornographic. I've taken many male models who have done *Playgirl*, and other agencies have

Detail
Body Study
Photo: Ken Haak

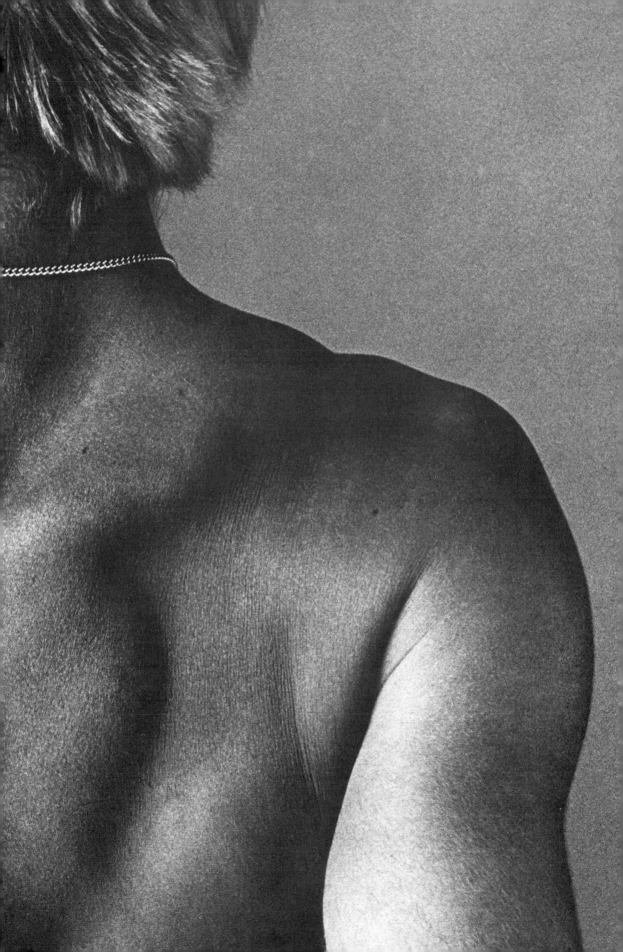

done the same, and the models have become very successful.

Asked if he would refuse to represent males who have appeared in *Blueboy*, the hugely popular gay magazine that often features men in semierect situations, he answers, "Not if they were terrific. No. No way. Because they'd outlive it and so would I."

Joey Hunter: "I don't think posing nude will affect a model's work at all. There may be certain clients, really straitlaced, who have prejudices and are afraid somebody will say, 'Isn't that the guy who was in *Blueboy* who's in your ad?' I know they would be very against that. But as far as me as an agent, if I thought the guy was good, I wouldn't worry about those clients. I'd tell the model up front that certain clients, if they saw the pictures, would not use him. But I would send him to the clients and let them worry about it. I don't feel I have to discuss somebody's past with a client. I'm not going to tell them."

It is common knowledge within the industry that several highly paid models have done nude work. Yet, in a protective gesture, most models and agents don't spread the word. Not one of the models who have literally exposed themselves would discuss the fact for attribution. Off-the-record is a different story.

"Carl Garrison," whose green eyes have stared from the cover of *GQ,* had done no professional modeling before posing as a "discovery." Usually diffident, he assumes a highly defensive attitude when references are made to a particular and, for him, controversial color spread. Although he achieved the transition into straight modeling speedily, sometimes he fears his "legit" bubble can be pricked and deflated. He is sometimes candid, then mercurially will become a skillful evader.

How do you feel about nude modeling?

"I don't mind it. I like the idea of it as long as it is done tastefully. I don't like to see a man lying there with his cock hanging between his legs hard as a rock. I think that is very ugly. But I don't think a man lying around or sitting or standing somewhere, if his body is halfway together, I don't see a damn thing wrong with it. I don't feel a man should be penalized because he has done something like that."

Were you punished or penalized?

"Yeah, I have been."

You have?

"Yeah, I lost a lot of jobs over it."

But you work all the time.

"I work all the time, yeah."

You say there have been repercussions?

"Yeah, because a few clients feel if a man has modeled in the nude, he isn't good enough to model their clothes. Because of what the old grandmothers might say in St. Louis."

What magazine did you model nude for?

"I wouldn't want that printed."

All right.

"Everyone knows about it anyway, but . . .""

Nobody is out to get you.

"I don't regret doing it. I never will. Because that was a part of my life. I did it and I wanted people to see it. But as far as clients not letting you work and losing jobs because of it, I think it's ridiculous. That grandmother in St. Louis who says, 'Who is this guy you're using? He has done a nude in *Playgirl* or somewhere like that? How disgusting!' I ask myself, 'How in the hell does she know I've done it unless she was out buying that magazine? So what the hell does she have to gripe about?' I've been on a shooting where people have come up to me and said, 'Are you the Carl Garrison that did so and so?' And I have to say yes. I can't say no. I can't lie to people. And they stopped the shooting. That happened to me."

How did that happen?

"The stylist knew who I was. She went and told the client. The client freaked out, right there on the set."

Have you lost much work?

"No. I mean, a lot of people know I've done it. They will come up and drop little hints. They know. But that doesn't bother me. I think a lot of times it has also helped, because a lot of people want to see me just because of that. It was a part of my life. I will never do it again."

You won't?

"No."

Would you do other kinds of nude modeling? An ad for a cologne or something like that?

"Yeah. If it were something like that, yes. You know, in the advertising world, that is part of it. But I would never get in front of a camera and take off my pants for a layout. For a magazine, no. Hell, I'm not ashamed of my body, and I don't see why anyone else should be either."

It's a paradox, isn't it? You can be nude in an ad and you might get more work because of it. That's standard and acceptable. But if you do a nudie magazine, you could lose work. It's still you and it's still your body.

"I've lost a lot of work—not a lot—but I've lost work over it."

Obviously it has not damaged your career.

"No, it hasn't damaged me. Maybe mentally. When that shooting comes up and the client says, 'Well, you didn't get the job because of that'—that kind of blows me away. It upsets me. It's like I am being punished for no reason. I'm proud of doing it. So is my mother. So is my grandmother."

Did it bother anyone you know personally?

"My father. He was pissed. He wrote me saying I had embarrassed the family. 'That is all right for any whore on the corner but . . .' He really let me have it."

Well, many models have done it. It's amazing how they won't own up to it out of fear that it might damage their careers.

"The magazines take advantage of you, too. They take the photos and they reuse them time after time. It's incredible. They put me on the cover of a hardcover book."

Without your permission? Oh, you had already signed the release.

"So they take advantage of you, really. But what are you going to do? There is nothing you can do. I don't want you to use my name in the book about this."

What name do you want?

"Robert Redford. I don't care. Sorry. Pick your own."

That accomplished, "Carl Garrison" is relaxed again.

Few male centerfold discoveries are fashion model material. Carl Garrison and the select others who have put their clothes back on to forge a career all possess the requisite suit size—40 regular or thereabouts—as well as a special look and a special drive. On the other hand, the requirements for nude modeling, as one auditioner for a male flesh magazine explains, are "body, face, cock," not necessarily in that order. "On the whole, most of the boys are pretty plain," notes a photographer for a gay publication, "and you have to create an illusion, a mystique about them in the photographs. And a lot of them aren't very dependable. You pick them up on the beach or wherever, and you set a time to shoot. You never know if they are going to show up."

Carl Garrison, when he was shot nude, had never entertained the notion of modeling; that idea came later at the urging of friends. Many of the fellows who pose for nude shots do so for the money or just for the hell of it. But often something clicks when the camera starts clicking: maybe they can make the transition into the "real" thing?

David (his true first name; his last withheld by request) is one of several *Blueboy* finds who aspire to a fashion-modeling career. He knows he will first need some costly dental work and is undaunted by the fact that he is 5 feet 10 inches, not 6 feet, and that, to date, no big model was born on those pages.

David is in his early twenties. He had been working as a night watchman when he was prodded by a friend of a friend to enter a Mr. Tampa contest in February 1978, which he describes as "a male beauty contest." As his talent, he worked out a robot disco routine to "Disco Inferno." He won. "I was really flying high," he says, recharged with delight. "I felt like I was a star." After the contest, he was introduced to an art director from *Blueboy*. "He said he wanted to do a shooting of me. Would I mind modeling nude for him? So I thought about it for a couple seconds, and I said, 'Well, let's try it and see. I've never done it before. You'll have to help me through because I don't know what I'm doing or nothing.' So, since then, I think I've had about three or four different shootings. It's something I like to do. It's enjoyable.

"The first shooting, I was very stiff. I tried to act like I thought models should look. And, like, when I went there, I had my hair blow-dried to a T, all in place, and about the first thing the photographer did was wet my hair all up. I'd make a pose and he'd say, 'No, no, loosen up, loosen up, you're too stiff.' We stopped and had a drink and talked. The first shooting, it was all right, but I wasn't what you would call professional at all. I was very nervous. I didn't know exactly what was going to come off and so I was standoffish at first. That first set was put out in *For Women Only*, a special magazine. I was one of the models in that. They used the name Pedro.

"The first time, I did it just for the money. Just something that would make me a little more money. Because I needed money at the time. But I found out that I really enjoyed it. The second shooting was right close to here. There were these big rock piles, rock and sand piles. It was right out on a busy intersection. And we did a shooting right there. We got nude shots and everything and there was millions of people around us and nobody knew what was going on. It was a neat experience. Have you ever been very close to a very busy intersction? A lot of people? But you're in a spot where you're alone. Right in the middle! And we were in that spot. Nobody ever knew what was going on. So it was really a far-out experience.

"What I enjoy about it is I'm knowing that other people are looking

"The first time, I did it just for the money," explains nude model "David." This head shot courtesy of Blueboy.

at me. And they're looking at me with sexual desires in their mind, so I kind of get off on myself, you know. Here I am, lying out there and I know somebody's going to look at that picture and really get turned on by it. And that turns me on a little bit. When I'm in that semierect state, I'm usually thinking of some kind of interlude that I've had. The position you're in, maybe you were in that position before with one of your partners. And then I figure how it was going on. I'm letting my mind drift and it catches a subject and then it comes through my eyes. That's where your sexiness comes from, really, it's not just looking at a body. It's looking at a face connected with a body.

"Sodoma," Blueboy *photographer,*
during session with "David."
Photos: Reinaldo Boza

"I don't think I'm the biggest in the world. But that's not what people looking at the pictures are looking for, I don't think. Like that expression, it's not how big you are, it's what you do with it. It's your feelings with each person. That doesn't really enter into it, my size. There are many people much bigger than me, much smaller than me. But someone smaller than me can be much more sexier than I am because it's all in the person. And a lot of times your rear end is used a lot more than your cock is. That might be the sexier part of your body. I'm not saying that some ugly people aren't fantastic to know. But this is a magazine they're trying to sell. Being a nude magazine, they want sexiness out of it. It's like a buildup: good-looking, oh, a nice body. Another level attained. Then a sexy cock, rear end, whatever.

"I've thought about doing movies. You know, porn. I've always been thinking about doing that from the beginning. Maybe in my mind it's a sexual turn-on to be photographed while I was in an interlude. It would not be what they call lovemaking. It would be sex. I think it would be a turn-on to me. I would like to do a movie. I don't think I could do one with an all-male cast. I'm into the female-male relationship, and I could do that. The other I couldn't.

"Modeling has changed me. It's opened up my mind a lot, especially with the touchy position that I'm in. It's not just taking pictures of me, it's taking pictures *of* me, just me, nude, in—what shall we call it?—a risqué position that the normal society will at times shun. The system we're in puts such a stereotype on everybody. If you're a nude model, you have to be different. You don't have feelings that other people have, which is totally wrong. I think in modeling you show your feelings. Your feelings, if they come out right in the pictures, are what make the pictures. So you're showing people that you do have feelings. Which is proving them wrong. Because I'm a nude model doesn't mean that I'm bad. If it bothers you, then don't look.

"I've never been rejected because I'm a nude model, but I know that it's going to come up. A lot of times, I don't talk about it to my friends because a lot of my friends are very straight and they would reject me. So I don't tell them about it. That part of my life is a closed door to them. They can open any door of my mind except that one. But there are some of my close friends that I tell what I'm doing, am able to, and at first they give you a little bit of coldness. But they realize that I'm still the person they like. I'm a close friend and that just happens to be part of me. And they accept it. Which is what anybody needs. Because rejection is nowhere for anybody.

"My mom is very religious and this type of thing to her would be what you call a gross sin. So I don't talk to her about it. But in essence, I think she knows. She's never confronted me because she doesn't really want to find out yes or no. My father, he knows nothing about it because I haven't seen him since my high school days. He left and I had to go to work.

"I like the nude shots, but my preference is fashion. I do enjoy fashion the most. I like to look good. I feel that I could sell clothes. I'm not really into selling my body or nothing. I would like to get into the field of modeling. We're putting together a portfolio for myself. I would like to move to New York or L.A. My suit size is a thirty-eight, but I have pretty broad shoulders. I don't think my height will hinder me that much. I'm five/ten, but I don't look that short. I look like an average man, about average height, average build and what-not. I enjoy modeling and it just happens that I'm photogenic and I'm better-looking in my pictures than I am in real life."

"John Rucculo" (a fictitious name selected by the former nude model himself) shares David's hope to move into legitimate modeling but refuses to do any more bare sessions. He has appeared on *Blueboy* covers twice, first munching on a green apple, and later drifting in a turquoise pool on a blue raft wearing a brilliant red swimming suit, a brilliant red sun visor and a brilliant white-toothed smile. On the latter cover, he bears an uncanny resemblance to John Travolta, for whom he's been mistaken several times. ("I don't think he's good-looking, so it's no thrill," says Rucculo.) Wearing wire-rimmed glasses, a plaid cowboy shirt and old dungarees, he looks less like the teen idol than does the magazine cover, which doesn't resemble the in-the-flesh personage all that much either. For one thing, he is much shorter than expected. "I'm short and stocky," Ruccolo says in self-description, comparing himself to "good models who are tall, slim, and have decent builds."

"John Ruccolo,"
portrait and cover.
Both courtesy of Blueboy.

His muscularity is the result of body building, an addiction. "It's hard to do. It's boring, but it strengthens your character, your willpower. You don't need to put anyone down. You don't have to smash into someone, like football. You're competing with yourself. And it's a conversation piece. Even if a chick thinks it's weird, ugly, whatever, you start talking."

Rucculo was working at a Miami health spa when a guy asked if he'd ever thought about modeling. "I think he was just a weirdo, in his forties or fifties, old in heart," he says. But the could-be weirdo mentioned *Blueboy*, which Rucculo was unfamiliar with. "When I found out it was a gay magazine, that didn't turn me on," he recalls. "It took me a long time to find a copy. A lot of stores just didn't carry it. So I figured no one would see it. Considering what it was, there wasn't anybody I could ask for counsel. But I needed some bread. I'm a drummer. As long as I have sticks in my hands, I'm happy. But there aren't always that many gigs, not every night. So I thought, I like anything new, so I called and all that. I hadn't intended to model nude. After shooting for five or six hours, the photographer said, 'Let's do the nude.' I said, 'Aw, fuck.' Before that, it was fun. But then I thought, 'A little poison won't kill; you can try anything.' And I did.

"When I found out that I was on the cover, at first I thought that was great. I wasn't just a fucking piece of meat in the middle of the magazine. But after a while I started to feel, 'I'm being used.' Sure, I was paid. But the release I signed gave them the right to do anything they wanted with those pictures. And, boy, have they used them. And *used* them. I feel exploited. I'm not sorry I did it. But I do think I should have been paid for all the times they used my pictures.

"I wouldn't do it again. And it isn't just the money. I would like to do other kinds of modeling, and I don't know if my doing that will hurt or not. I don't think so. Now, in twenty years, if I were to be a congressman, I know it would hurt. But I'm going to be in the arts—music, acting, modeling or body building (I think that's an art). So I don't think it will hurt and maybe it will help. As far as anyone else is concerned, I don't give a fuck. There are a lot of unhappy people in this world who have to pick on someone.

"The main thing, it was too easy. To do that, you don't need a composite, you don't need any talent. It's nothing to be proud of. It's no big deal, but it's nothing to be proud of. If I model, I want it to be me, not just someone who can take his clothes off. I've seen some of the guys they've photographed. They look like derelicts. Scum. I started on the bottom. I don't want to stay on the bottom. No one in my family has seen it, and I hope they won't until I move out. I think my father would kick me out."

Michael Monahan is exceptional for several reasons. First, that's his true name. Second, his mother knows about the nude shooting he did for *Blueboy*. ("I just told her straight out," he says. "She went out and got about ten copies. She shows them to everybody. She keeps the photos in the living room, on the wall. Well, the cover and a couple others. The nude she will not display because of my little sisters. That page she kept closed. She just didn't want to see that.") Third, Monahan is openly gay. ("Before I came out, I was a real pain. Always in trouble. I was on probation. Always locked up. Always getting into something. I was getting screwed up in the head all the time. When I came out, when I started going and meeting different people, it just like snapped something in me. I've taken my mother to the bars and she likes them better than the straight bars because the people are a lot friendlier. My mother can see I'm having a lot more fun than I would

Michael Monahan was named
Sean in his nude spread.
Photo courtesy of Blueboy.

probably any other way. She's happy with it. She's very happy. I'll do anything for gays. I'm one person who jumps in. It doesn't bother me if others don't like it. It just shows what they are. Not human.")

When he was twenty, Monahan left Cleveland ("Just to get away from Cleveland." He laughs. "You don't need to ask why.") and headed for Key Largo. A friend proposed he contact *Blueboy*. Monahan offers the usual explanation of why he acted on the suggestion: "At the time, I needed the money." But he tacks on another rationale as well: "I figured I could get some recognition from it. It's kind of nice to have a little popularity going." He also hoped that an agent or producer might see the spread, that he might be offered an acting role. If such a figure were magically to materialize, did he ever consider he might be pursued for other reasons? "That went across my mind. Especially when the photographer took the picture. Because of the angle, it made me look bigger. I didn't really like that part, I didn't get off on that. I selected the pictures I wanted the magazine to use. They didn't; the pictures weren't at that angle. The others were more like me.

"I wanted people to look at the shots and say, 'That is a very nice picture and that is a very nice-looking person.' I don't need them going into the bathroom for an hour with the magazine and coming out with the pictures stuck together. That's kind of sick. I didn't do it for an ego thing, like to say, 'Well, I've got a beautiful body,' and everything like that. Because I'm not perfect and I know that.

"I don't like the pictures. I don't. It's just not the way I would have liked to be photographed. I wanted it outdoors—like out by the beach, more like in the country with horses—not in somebody's living room.

"Besides, *Blueboy* used a different name with my photos. They called me Sean. I really wanted my own name. But there's nothing I can do about that now. I did sign the contract.

"And they didn't pay me very much. I think I should have gotten more. They were paying fifty dollars an hour, but for a centerfold and a cover, I think you should get more. But they did it the regular way, paying the same amount no matter what the spread was. And when you sign the contract, they can sell those pictures to anybody they want to. I figure they made a lot more off me than I did. And I would have liked to have made more, because it sure would help. I wouldn't work for them again. I would tell them I want more an hour, and they probably wouldn't agree to it. So I probably wouldn't have the chance of doing it again. But, if I do more modeling and, you know, I am getting to be known, if I lost my career over what I've done or what I am, that's fine. I mean, because I would have started from that. I could end up just like that. It is no problem for me. Really."

"Ralph" (back to pseudonyms) is yet another nude model who hopes to turn legitimate, although his most prominent pictures didn't appear in *Blueboy*. Unlike David, John and Michael, he has parlayed his physical endowments into another plateau of nude modeling. First, back to the beginning. Typically, he felt he could use some extra, non-taxable bucks. He noticed an ad in a newspaper calling for nude male models.

"I had confidence that I had a good enough looking face and privately I had confidence that I was well hung," relates Ralph, son of a clergyman. "At the same time I didn't know if it would bring any real revenue in. I decided to make a stab at it, so I called and was given a time to come in for an interview. There were about four or five other guys in the waiting room. Everybody just looked at the floor, you know? They had a lot of magazines spread out, *U.S. News & World Report, Business Week* and a couple family magazines thrown in. No nude magazines. One or two guys left. They got real fidgety and left. I was sitting there comparing myself to this guy and that guy. A black guy in a jump suit came in. He smoked one cigarette after another. After he was there about five minutes, this black girl walked in and said, 'Are you ready?' And he said, 'No, I'll wait longer.' The second time she walked in, they had a little conversation in a whisper. The third time she came in, he walked out with her. Then it was my turn to go in. The guy was real friendly. He said he'd need a couple Polaroids. I just took my pants off. I wanted to leave my shirt on. He said, 'Well, I'll just leave you here in the room for a few minutes and see if you can get a little hard.' Cause when you've been working all day, whatever you've been doing, coming in there, you're nervous and you're scared, your genitals kind of shrivel up. It didn't look like I had much. But I knew I had more and I was trying to show him, right? So he gave me time in the room, privately closed the door. I tried to work it up, you know, and nothing happened. So he walked back in a little later and looked again and watched me jerking off. Nothing was happening. The third time he walked in, I was about ready to give up. But I got a little bit going there and he said it was enough and he took a few pictures. He said they'd be confidential, that I didn't have to worry about that. I had concerns about my parents, my sisters, my friends, that they would ever see stuff like that. I felt guilty, you know? He left the room. I pulled my pants up and I left.

"A week later I received a call. 'There's a guy coming down in a week. Can we arrange a time to set up an interview?' I was very skeptical. Suppose I got out in the woods and he pulls a gun on me. Or he pulls a knife on me. I don't know who this guy is. Sure, I'll do something for money, because that's what everybody wants in life. But what if this guy is crazy? But the interview was going to be in a business office. I took an afternoon off from my job—I was working as a social worker then—and got all prepared for it, got dressed up and went down. The photographer was very, very nice. He was a young guy, with an assistant who was also there and was also very nice. They asked to see what I had and I showed them, working it up a little. When it came down to actually setting up a time to do some shooting, that scared the shit out of me. I realized, I am going to do it, I'm actually going to pull my pants down in front of a camera.

"Actually, the day ended up beautiful. I enjoyed it. In fact, I got really into it. I'm self-sexual. I mean, I'm heterosexual, but I'm also self-sexual. I got high on a reefer. I had pretty decent success at getting it up. They let me do what I wanted. I took my flippers and mask and scuba gear out there. They took some pictures of me on the dock preparing to go into the water. And then they did some scenes with me, just lying there on the dock with a hard-on. They promised me they wouldn't use any pictures in the magazine when I was hard. I was getting it hard because I was trying to make it big, but I didn't want to have it look hard, because I thought at the time that maybe I was doing something illegal. I was scared as shit. But they relaxed me. I felt relaxed and realized that they were good people. And I began to look at it as a business. I really got into it that first day.

"Well, the two photographers were young and inexperienced. I looked terrible. But I got paid two hundred dollars."

Since then, Ralph has graduated into more soft and not-so-soft—in fact hard—porn, including a movie. He is preoccupied with techniques to maintain an on-going erection. He also claims a preoccupation with getting together a reputable portfolio and initiating a new career in fashion modeling. At best, his chances are slim.

"There are nudes that are done for ads or a few things like that that won't hurt a guy," pronounces Nina Blanchard. "But you get back to the old business about prurient interest. That's really what we're talking about. I have no quarrel with nudity. I have no quarrel with anything grown-ups do as long as they don't trespass on me or on children. What consenting adults do in private is one thing. Porno magazines are another. Let any adult in the world look at them. As long as they're not looking at any of my models in them."

The disapproval engendered by nude modeling spills over into the world of straight modeling, though to a lesser degree, merely because the root word "model" is used in both cases. "Model" is also a euphemism for an entirely different profession, as evidenced by an ad (quoted verbatim, minus telephone number) that appeared in the classified section of a gay publication called *Florida Knight Life*. "Ft. Lauderdale—Young versatile models Bob & Michael available in your home or ours. Call anytime."

Asked his reaction to the misappropriation of the term "model" by men more intent on hustling, Bill Loock is pragmatic and philosophical: "There's nothing to be done about it. It's like the hooker who's arrested and her occupation in the newspaper articles is listed as model. I don't like it, but I'm certainly not going to worry about it. Modeling is a very legitimate business. Everybody has heard stories, which aren't true. You don't have to do anything in this business except stand in front of a camera and do it right. People are always willing to think the worst. But not as much now as when I started out."

Although the misunderstandings are less frequent, they persist nonetheless. The on-going judgment against models—legitimate or nude—is that the work is not moral, is not "good" work. It's not as immoral as that of their impersonators' field of specialization, even the most adamant disclaimers of models concede. Models are not real whores, but they do sell their bodies, upright souls point out. So do ditch diggers.

While many models will balk at the comparison, reading between the lines during a conversation with a self-styled Dream Lover illustrates how a bright, possibly courageous, certainly unpretentious, flesh peddler and how legitimate models must all ultimately choose their own wave and ride it.

The voice: Jack Wrangler. He has taken his own body and built a gainful enterprise out of it. Although he sells sex, he insists he has never put himself up for grabs: never has he exchanged personal favors for payment, although he has performed explicitly for cameras. Interestingly, he never seeks justification for his chosen career in terms of dollars earned, although he rakes in more than many top professional models. His reward? Believe it or not, his self-esteem. And, if you were to meet him and talk to him without first closing your mind, believe it or not, you'd believe he's telling the truth. Or that he believes he is. Possibly he's fooling himself. If he's self-deluding, he's an expert at that art. If he doesn't believe his words, he's a consummate actor and deceiver. Wrangler has seen his hair turn white and then blond again through artifice. But his demeanor during the interview is devoid of artifice. He is not the hard-fucking screen personality. He is that unusual phenomenon, a truly gentle man.

What is your career?

"To most of the public, I'm the most well-known male porno star in the world. That has built into a lot of merchandising spinoffs, like the Jack Wrangler Fraternity Travel Club and others, all through Wrangler Corporation. Basically, I make about six or seven films a year, X-rated films. Both heterosexual and gay. I started out just making gay ones and then I expanded into the heterosexual market.

How long have you been in, what you call, the X-rated industry?

"Four years."

What were you doing before that?

"I went to Northwestern University. While I was there I worked for the Ivanhoe Theatre and played the juvenile in all those comedies. They were all star-system things, all built around the star, the personality, not the play. After I finished college, I went right on with a star, with Hermione Gingold. We were doing a show called *Dear Charles.* Then I went to Texas and ended up doing seventeen star-system plays for one theater there. I had a clever manager who said, 'Jack, don't do another show until you can direct.' So the first show I directed was Gale Storm in *Plaza Suite*. Then I directed for almost seven years after that, one show after another, and also had a chain of theaters. What happened was, I was asked to do a play in San Francisco called *Special Friends*. It was a comedy, and it was a nonunion show. I couldn't use my real name. I had been fined by the union before and they not only fine you but make you go to a dreadful meeting which is worse than the fine. I didn't want to be fined again, so the night before the program was going to press, I was wearing a Wrangler work shirt and I said, 'Call me Jack Wrangler.' So they did and they said I was from Minnesota and I wanted to be a forest ranger. And if the play didn't succeed, I could go back to the trees. But the play did succeed. It won the Drama Critics Award for 1974, I guess, and I also won the best actor of 1974 by the San Francisco County Performing Arts. In the show I took my shirt off. All of a sudden there were pictures and covers and centerfolds for everything all over the United States. And everybody had heard of Jack Wrangler. So that is how the character—Jack Wrangler—happened. I think I've become more him over the last few years. In the play he was a dumb ass from Arkansas, a very fifties sort of guy. He believes in figureheads and God and Mom and Apple Pie and all that. He is very much boy-next-door. That character and his inner strength caught on on the screen."

Why did you break with the legitimate theater?

"I think it was a combination of things. I wanted to be a personality. I had always been a working actor. But I didn't want to be a working actor. I wanted to be known as Jack Wrangler, whether I was another character in a play or film or whatever. I wanted to be an identifiable personality. Because I thought it would be more fun, frankly.

"I grew up in the Hollywood/Beverly Hills syndrome. I was surrounded by beautiful people all my life and people who were acclaimed all over the world as internationally beautiful people. I did not consider myself a part of that. They were in my house but I was not one of them. And I think there was a great need to feel physically desired, based on insecurity. An exhibitionist is one who is very proud of his body and wants to show it off. It is completely opposite with me. I was so insecure with mine that I wanted to build myself into something that everyone would say was beautiful whether I believed it or not.

"Having decided to become Wrangler, first of all I went and talked to my parents about it. They are both in show business and I always confide in them whenever I am going to make a move in the entertainment business. My parents had always been against this whole hypocritical morality syndrome in the first place. My parents said, 'Look, go into it, but if you do, be sure you are the top of it and always anticipate your next chess move.'

"I knew that doing X-rated films can severely limit you. First of all, you are immediately aced out of doing television commercials, soap

operas, anything where middle America is going to get its dander up because—'For heaven's sake, this man actually takes his clothes off on-screen and commits actual sexual acts.' So I had to go into it with my eyes open, knowing this was going to happen."

Why were you willing to take the risk?

"Because I thought my timing was right. The first thing I did was a stage appearance. I appeared on stage as Jack Wrangler, in Los Angeles at a theater which has since burned to the ground. They had a policy of having go-go dancers. And I didn't dance. Also, I didn't think that a person's fantasy image of an ideal man really incorporated his dancing in front of you. So the first thing I did was walk downstage as Jack Wrangler, wearing a work shirt and Levis, stood there and smoked a cigarette. I had a lot of clothes on because I thought: What else the hell am I going to do? I completely shut out the audience, only because I am nearsighted. I imagined I was on a mountaintop and I was alone and I was just getting off on the beauty and ruggedness of it. So eventually my shirt came off and I started discovering my body, becoming one with the landscape. They loved it because suddenly they saw somebody having a very private moment. They got to watch me being alive. *I* wasn't entertaining them. I was a character. That was the first thing. Then I did a magazine in which I did have hard-ons and all that stuff."

Did you ever have aspirations connected with legitimate modeling?

"Yeah, I did, but all the doors were really closed for me in that area. First of all, at that time I was a very skinny kid. I had started working out in a gym because I knew that to become Wrangler I was going to have to really build myself up over a period of time. But I really wasn't a good type for fashion modeling. I was smart enough to know it. First

Jack Wrangler (top left) porn star; (center)
earlier in his career as a legitimate actor;
(right) a recent portrait by Joel Kudler.

of all, I am five feet seven and a half inches tall, which is bad, and I am not a standard forty and I am not any of the things that one really needs to be a model, not to be the tops."

How did you learn your craft when you started doing nude shots?

"I used my knowledge as an actor, the personal excitement and involvement with my body. It was more expression, the eyes. As far as the look I wanted to have, I did not go through magazines. I invented my own. The flannel shirt/Levi thing hadn't even come into being then. I really started that. I mainly started that because I was endorsing a clothing store called Intermountain Logging Company and all they had was flannel shirts and Levis. So I started wearing them a lot and so did everyone else.

"I love the character of Wrangler. He's a nice and an interesting guy. And he's a guy that maybe I wanted to be. I like becoming him. The voice changes, the walk changes, the face changes, everything changes. It's like a long run of a show. I've been playing this character for a long time. It's like two people. It's like schizophrenia."

How many films have you done?

"I just did my seventy-ninth feature. And I've done hundreds of mail-order eight-millimeters and thousands of magazines. So almost every day I'm shooting on something. There has to be a better way of putting that —actually, it is a very accurate way of putting that."

Do you have any funny stories?

"Any shooting I have ever done, something wild has happened. Like I was doing this very heavy fight scene. I had to leap at the guy and throw him down to the ground. And I was dragged around. We were fighting all over the place, rolling down hills and rocks. I went through a whole ocean of poison oak on the first day of shooting. I was literally covered with poison oak, every part of my body, and we had to work with that.

"Another time, we were working in a boat. We get out to sea and the models who had been very indifferent to one another up to then began looking very hungrily at each other. It wasn't passionate. It was time for lunch. When I'm at home, I really watch my food intake. But on locations all you ever get is cheeseburgers, pickles and onions. And after making six or seven of these cheeseburgers, pickles and onions, I began to realize that all the models tasted alike. And so I started bringing along Lavoris. Now all the models still taste alike, but better. Lunch, Lavoris. It's time to go back to work. My two friends started getting it on and I was downstairs and all of a sudden this ship appeared next to ours. It turned out to be a Girl Scout camp on their annual outing to study rare forms of marine biology."

Do models make careers in nude modeling?

"Not unless they are personalities and names. Different magazines make blanket deals and contracts. I have heard about some of those contracts and they sound pretty frightening. You start making money when you start making films. Even then, most models are paid very little unless they are a name."

Can they make a living out of nude modeling?

"Not without endorsements or something. It's a very limited field."

Why do most men go into it?

"One, because they need some bucks and somebody offers them a hundred bucks or so if they will pose nude for them. The same reason some people might end up in prostitution. They figure they are going to do it once and forget it."

Any other reasons?

"Sure. It really means a lot to them for the public to see them nude. To be respected as a sexual object. I know a lot of actors who have done it not just for the money but because they needed to be able to really strip themselves. Some people actually have philosophical reasons. They feel that man is the only animal with the ability to fantasize and that to deny ourselves that right would be denying something that makes us strictly human. But once they have done it, a lot of people hate it because they can't cope with it."

What can't they cope with?

"Well, because people accost you on the street (often in a friendly manner) or at the theater or anyplace you go. Even with those who are very kind and nice and charming—you feel everybody is undressing you.

Does that come as a surprise?

"No. If it does, you're pretty stupid."

Would you advise anyone to do nude modeling as a steppingstone into a legitimate career?

"Absolutely not. There are a lot of companies, film companies as well, especially when commercials are involved, that won't hire you if you have done nude modeling whether it was for *Playgirl* or for *Playboy* or whatever.

"That question triggers something else. A person should never go into nude modeling unless he really has his head together. Face it, there's a stigma attached to it. It's financially risky, as well as personally. Spending all your time worrying about your body and your face can be very limiting—you never are allowed to really grow. Of course, it's a very short-lived thing, and the terror of age can be frightening to the extent you can get suicidal. But there are valid reasons for doing it. Now, I find myself much more confident as an actor on stage. Wrangler doesn't have to go on a cattle call. He very seldom has to audition. Even for legit things now. I needed one extra thing to give me a strike on stage which I never really had. It was knowing I am a turn-on to millions of people.

"I would never want to say I wouldn't recommend it. There are a lot of cards stacked against you. For me, it worked. And I am delighted that I did it. I would have missed something wonderful if I had not done it."

summing up

After I'd completed the first draft of this book, I took a breather from the typewriter and reread all the transcripts of the models interviewed. Sometimes my stomach knotted. I thought I had retrieved all the truly vital pieces, but now and again I would rediscover an amusing anecdote or a wise statement I hadn't included. Or I would remember a tone of voice, a precise gesture that I had not recorded, and could not record in words. Reading through the pages again, I was reminded that I was writing about these men's lives as well as their profession. They had told me intimate feelings, not merely objective facts; they had recounted interrelated episodes and complex changes of events, yet I was quoting only a sentence here, a paragraph there, trying to paint with those words a coherent picture of a whole industry. Sometimes I felt I had diminished them in an attempt to describe the phenomenon called Male Modeling. But I did not interview archetypes, I interviewed men. They were who they are. One asked me to hide the tape recorder. One asked for vodka on the rocks. One had laryngitis. Some were silly, some were witty, others were windbags, a couple were evasive, a few argumentative, and most were vulnerable. Rereading their words, I saw more clearly that the reason they wanted to talk was to explain themselves as people, not as models. They wanted their individual voices to be heard.

Every fellow interviewed thought that his story was unique. And every fellow was right. A twist or a turn always distinguished his experiences from another's. Certain patterns could be discerned, but the men were more different than alike. They might say similar things or express similar feelings, but the rhythm of their words, the juxtaposition of phrases, emphasized their diversity.

187

I wondered if I were attempting an impossibility. Could bits and pieces from all their stories be fitted together in a continuous narrative to represent all of their experiences? Nope. But using their statements, maybe I could show that our society has unjustly assumed that all male models are alike. Individuals can suffocate beneath the weight of stereotypes. Every victim wants to breathe freer. What I couldn't do for the men individually (I couldn't write biographies of some sixty men) I'd attempt to do collectively—smash the stereotypes. Their words, as severely edited as they necessarily had to be, could do that. And I'd employ my own to the same end.

The two-dimensional view of male models is intimately tied to the nature of their work. They are assigned the task of depicting the American Male in one form or another. Our most vigorous criticism of male models—that they *don't* represent the American Male—is flabby and archaic. Who could? No one. The American Male is a myth, just as the Male Model is a myth. Statistically, we can establish the average age, the median income, the educational background, plus all sorts of esoteric data about the American Male, but what do we end up with? An abstraction. Nothing of flesh, of spirit. We could do the same for the Male Model. Statistically, the results would be different, of course, but the composite would nonetheless only be another bloodless abstraction. In our attempts to see the larger picture, we often overlook the human details. Minus the capital letters, any man or any male model is representative of no one other than himself.

Although I found that most models were interested in justifying themselves (understandably, given the amount of criticism heaped upon them), I ran into a pitfall of my own. I wanted to vindicate the men, true, but not the profession. As a profession, it deserves neither special praise nor special damnation. By virtue of his profession, a janitor is no less and no more worthy than a judge. By virtue of his profession, a model is not necessarily better or worse than a janitor, a judge or anyone else. There are no honorable professions, only honorable men.

How male modeling will evolve is open to numerous guesses. Some observers believe we'll soon see a surge of models who look like "real people" (that phrase again). If so, how unfortunate for us all. Why must we all be average, the same? Why shouldn't we be extraordinary? Besides, the concept of "real people" is an oversimplification, for many of *them* (that is, *us*) are extraordinary. We must see beauty in all people to see it in ourselves.

Michael Taylor, today
Photo: Les Goldberg

INDEX

Bold numerals indicate model photographs